This book is a

Gift

From

....

To

....

Date

....

May God bless you through this book

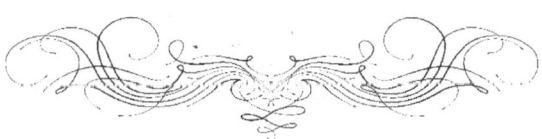

INTERNATIONAL WOMEN'S PRAYER NETWORK – PRAYER M. MADUEKE

INTERNATIONAL WOMEN'S PRAYER NETWORK

PRAYER M. MADUEKE

PRAYER PUBLICATIONS
15, Olumo Street, Onike, Yaba, Lagos State, Nigeria.
46, Adelabu Street, Uwani, Enugu State,
Nigeria.
+234 803 353 0599

INTERNATIONAL WOMEN'S PRAYER NETWORK

Copyright © 2018

ISBN: 9781986064026

PRAYER M. MADUEKE

Prayer Publications

All rights reserved. No part of this work may be reproduced or transmitted in any form or by any means without written permission from the publisher

Unless otherwise indicated, all Scripture quotations are taken from the King James Version of the Bible, and used by permission. All emphasis within quotations is the author's additions.

First Edition, 2018

For further information of permission
15, Olumo Street, Onike, Yaba, Lagos State Nigeria.

46, Adelabu Street, Uwani, Enugu State, Nigeria.
+234 803 353 0599
Email: prayermadu@yahoo.com,
Website: www.prayermadueke.com

An Invitation to Become a Ministry Partner

In response to several calls from readers of my books on how to partner with this ministry, we are grateful to provide our ministry's bank details.

Be assured that our continued prayers for you will be answered according to God's word. And as you remain faithful by sowing seeds of faith, God will never forget your labors of love in Christ.

IN NIGERIA & AFRICA

Send your seed to:

Bank: Access Bank

Account Name: Prayer Emancipation Missions

Account Number: 0692638220

IN THE UNITED STATES AND THE REST OF THE WORLD

Bank: Wells Fargo - Bank

Account Name: Madueke P Madueke

Account Number: 7661203070

Routing Number (RTN): 055003201

DEDICATION

This book is first; dedicated to God the Father, Son and God the Holy Spirit. Secondly, it is dedicated to Umuadaigbo, every women's ministry, all women ministers, sisters' fellowship and women worldwide. This is in recognition for the positive contributions of all the model women in the past and present generation. God bless the women, I stand with you.

INTERNATIONAL WOMEN'S PRAYER NETWORK – PRAYER M. MADUEKE

Table of Contents

GOD'S PURPOSE FOR CREATING WOMEN 14

ATTACKS AGAINST WOMEN 21

    14 ACTIONS OF UNLIBERATED WOMEN 33

THE WOMAN THAT SITS UPON MANY WATERS 36

QUALITIES OF OVERCOMERS AMONG WOMEN 55

THE RAPTURE OF THE SAINTS 69

    HOW IT WILL HAPPEN 70

THE TRUTH ABOUT THE RAPTURE 70

THE REASON FOR THE RAPTURE 72

QUALIFICATION TO BE RAPTURED 73

THE JUDGMENT SEAT OF GOD OR BEMA 74

THE JUDGMENT EXPLAINED 75

TYPES OF REWARDS 77

THE PROPER MARRIGE 78

GREAT TRIBULATION 80

THE NATURE OF GREAT TRIBULATION 82

THE PURPOSE OF THE GREAT TRIBULATION 83

THE SOURCE OF THE GREAT TRIBULATION 84

HOW LONG WILL GREAT TRIBULATION LAST? 85

EXPOSING ANTICHRIST, THE BEAST 86

ADVICE TO TRIBULATION SAINTS 87

ANTICHRIST, THE KING OF FIERCE COUNTENANCE 87

NAMES AND TITLES OF ANTICHRIST 88

REVELATIONAL FACTS CONCERNING ANTICHRIST'S ACTIVITIES .89

WHO IS HE, OR HINDERING HIM? 90

THE SECOND COMING (ADVENT) OF CHRIST 95

THE BATTLE OF ARMAGEDDON 97

THE DEVASTATION BY THE CONQUEROR 98

THE RESURRECTION TO LIFE OR THE FIRST RESSURRECTION .. 100

EXAMPLES OF RESURRECTION 101

SECOND, DAMNATION, OR RESURRECTION OF THE UNSAVED 103

THE MILLENNIAL REIGN OF CHRIST 104

ARREST AND CONFINEMENT OF SATAN 107

CHRISTS REIGN WITH THE SAINTS ON EARTH 108

DELIVERANCE WITHOUT SALVATION 109

THE GREAT WHITE THRONE JUDGMENT 111

THE FAITHFUL JUDGE 112

THE BOOKS OF RECORD 112

THE BOOK OF LIFE 113

COMPREHENSIVE JUSTICE 114

HELL, THE DESTINY OF SINNERS 115

THE REALITY OF HELL 116

WHAT JESUS SAID ABOUT HELL 117

WHAT IS THE LAKE OF FIRE? 118

THE NEW HEAVEN AND NEW EARTH 119

DIVINE PROGRAM OUTLINE 119

SETTING THE PACE FOR THE NEW WORLD 120

OPPORTUNITY FOR NEW RELATIONSHIP 121

REWARDS FOR BELIEVERS AND PUNISHMENT TO THE REBELS 121

THINGS TRUE OVER COMERS MUST OVERCOME 122

DESCRIPTION AND INHERITANCE IN NEW JERUSALEM 123

THE GLIMPSE OF THE EVERLASTING CITY 124

EXCLUSION FROM THE CITY 125

THE INHABITANTS OF THE CITY 126

LIFE IN THE NEW CITY 126

THE LIFESTYLE IN HEAVEN 127

NATURE OF THE CITY 128

MEASUREMENT AND SIZE OF THE CITY 129

HERITAGE RECEIVED FROM GOD 130

IT IS IMPOSSIBLE TO PROFANE THE CITY 131

URGENT NEED FOR REVIVAL 131

WHY DO WE NEED REVIVAL? 132

MEANS OF REVIVAL 135

PRICE OF REVIVAL 136

BENEFITS OF REVIVAL 136

THINGS PRAYER CAN DO 138

Warfare Section

PRAYERS TO OVERCOME SATAN AND WARS 148

DEALING WITH MARRIAGE DESTROYERS 150

BREAKING EVIL MARRIAGES 155

TOTAL FREEDOM FROM LEVIATHAN 157

Victory Over Marine Witchcraft 159

Leviathan Must Die!!! 161

War Against Dream Criminals 163

Operations Of The Woman That Sits Upon The Waters
.... 165

Unseating The Evil Woman 167

Disgracing The Great Prostitute 169

Mystery Of The Evil Woman Exposed 171

Judgement Against The Prostitute 173

Battle Techniques Against The Evil Woman 175

Carying The Blood Of Jesus To The Foundation 177

Boiling The Water Against Marine Powers 179

Spirit Of My Parent Living Inside Me, Come Out 181

Prayer To Get Married Happily 183

Prayers To Destroy Marital Delay 185

Prayers To Meet And Marry My Man 188

Wars, Battles And Troubles In My Marriage, End 190

Power To Conceive And Bear Children 192

Deliverance From Divorce In Marriage 194

Victory Over The Enemies Of The Year 196

GOD'S PURPOSE FOR CREATING WOMEN

The first person that God created is man called Adam, formed out of the dust of the ground without life. Later, God breathed into the nostrils of man the breath of life, and he became a living soul. He also created employment for man, and thereafter, handed the whole creation to man.

And the LORD God took the man, and put him into the garden of Eden to dress it and to keep it. – **Genesis 2:15-17**

Though, man had a job, breath of God's life, a beautiful garden to dress and keep with everything good on earth willed to him as a personal inheritance from God, he was not happy. God discovered that everything on earth, though good, were not good enough to satisfy Adam without a woman. In order to make man's stay on earth good and satisfactory, the woman had to get involved in the affairs of man. God caused Adam to go into deep sleep, and while he was sleeping, God took one of his ribs and closed it up with his flesh. He used the rib to make the woman and brought her to Adam. When Adam saw the woman, he called her "the bone of my bones and the flesh of my flesh. Right there, Adam called her woman because she was taken out of man.

And the LORD God said, it is not good that the man should be alone; I will make him an help meet for him… And Adam gave names to all cattle, and to the fowl of the air, and to every beast of the field; but for Adam there was not found an help meet for him…Therefore shall a man leave his father and his mother, and shall cleave unto his wife: and they shall be one flesh. – **Genesis 2:18, 20, 24**

From the beginning, God's plan for creating male and female was for marriage. But his purpose for creating woman in particular is to make a man feel good and to overcome loneliness. Though everything God created is good, but the goodness in them was not enough to make man completely feel good the way God wanted. Women are help mates for men in order for man to fulfil God's purpose and assignment on earth (Genesis2:15-20).

THE ASSIGNMENT OF WOMEN INCLUDES:

✓ To have a job, a garden to dress and keep clean and holy to prevent the serpent from encroaching into it in the absence of her husband.

✓ Also, to help man obey God; encourage him to keep his commandment, and avoid eating from the tree of knowledge.

✓ It also includes staying with the man, watching over him, making him happy, and remaining forever with him as long as they live; like bone to the flesh and flesh to the bone.

✓ To cleave, remain united in plan and purpose, and be obedient to God's command as long as they are both alive.

✓ To help man to retain God's image, character and nature as God created man to be.

✓ To remain in his blessings and to continue in it.

✓ To be fruitful, multiply, replenish the earth, subdue it and have dominion over other creatures, including the devil.

Based on the above, I tell you, no man can go to heaven without the help of his wife and no nation go to hell if the women refuse to lead.

So God created man in his own image, in the image of God created he him; male and female created he them. And God blessed them, and God said unto them, be fruitful, and multiply, and replenish the earth, and subdue it: and have dominion over the fish of the sea, and over the fowl of the air, and over every living thing that moveth upon the earth. – **Genesis 1:27-28**

✓ To fulfil destiny, God's purpose on earth, and live holy.

A man and woman need to come together in a holy marriage. It brings their labors in life with good reward; nothing less. It can keep a man from falling and deliver a man who has fallen already. Good marriage is better than staying alone even with the best wealth on earth put together. When a man and woman are united in marriage by God, no power can prevail over them as long as they obey God's commandment. No matter where they lay together, the heat from their unity will warm them and empower them to fight and win every battle. If one gets weak in any of life's battle, their unity will turn the table and convert their defeats to victories.

Two are better than one; because they have a good reward for their labour. For if they fall, the one will lift up his fellow: but woe to him that is alone when he falleth; for he hath not another to help him up. Again, if two lie together, then they have heat: but how can one be warm alone? And if one prevail against him, two shall withstand him; and a threefold cord is not quickly broken. – **Ecclesiastes 4:9-12**

A united husband and wife cannot be consumed by war, no matter who is involved; even the whole creature, including the devil. Such holy, united and obedient couple will have godly seeds as long as they refuse to deal treacherously against each other.

And did not he make one? Yet had he the residue of the spirit. And wherefore one? That he might seek a godly seed. Therefore take heed to your spirit, and let none deal treacherously against the wife of his youth. – **Malachi 2:15**

A good marriage kills sexual sins, keep families, communities and nations together and holy.

ATTACKS AGAINST WOMEN

What happened to Eve in the garden, their residence was very unfortunate and regrettable. She kept the garden un-kept, undressed, in shambles, and unprotected in the absence of her husband, Adam. The entrance doors were opened and unlocked, and in addition, she failed to use her power and authority to subdue her enemy. Instead, she accepted an evil visitor right into her matrimonial home without her husband's permission. She allowed the devil into her matrimonial bed, gave him her husband's place, and relaxed with an enemy of God.

What really happened? Did she commit immorality with the devil? I do not know. We have to stop where the scripture stopped. All I know is that she disobeyed a simple command, *"Thou shalt not eat the tree of the knowledge of good and evil."*

That is the mistake of many today. The mistake and the disobedience was that she listened to the lies of the serpent, looked thoughtfully at the forbidden fruit, doubted God, desired what God prohibited, acted against God's word, became a sinner and a tempter, and brought the whole world into bondage (Genesis 3:1-7).

The relationship brought female and male demons into human relationship on earth today. The consequence caused all human beings, male and female, to inherit sinful nature (Romans 12:19; Psalms 51:5; Romans 3:9-10; 7:14-21). Everyone on earth became guilty of sin (Romans 3:19; John 3:18, 36). Because that relationship allowed the devil to come into the garden, the marital bedroom, he refused to leave. That is why many people, single and married, are having problems right from their homes.

But while men slept, his enemy came and sowed tares among the wheat, and went his way. – **Matthew 13:25**

This evil power allowed by Adam and Eve are still around planting hatreds, misunderstanding, fighting, disagreements, sexual perversion, wickedness, fornication, covetousness, malice, envy, deceits, pride, boastings, evil inventions, unmerciful lifestyle, lesbianism, homosexual, intimidating fear against doing the right things, lack of God's fears, sorceries, idolatry, cultism, lying and hating God. All these evil characters are planted while men sleep or cooperate with the devil to sin against God and disobey his word by doing abominable things.

Who are these enemies that move around, entering people's locked-up houses to plant evil characters and all manner of problem? They are evil spirits; fallen angels chased out of heaven for disobedience. Their leader is the devil, the serpent, the accuser of brethren, adversary, Abaddon, Beelzebub, Dragon, the father of lies, liar, Lucifer, the god of this world, prince of this world, prince of the devil, prince of the power of the air, ruler of darkness, sinner and murderer. It is because of his activities on earth that the scriptures called him these names (Revelation 12:10; 1 Peter 5:8; Revelation 9:11; Matthew 12:24; Revelation 17:3; John 8:44' 14:12; 2 Corinthians 4:4; Revelation 12:9; John 14:30; Matthew 12:24; Ephesians 2:2; 6:12; 1 John 3:8; 8:44).

Both believers in the time of Christ and the apostles with divine eyeglasses saw these evil forces moving from house to house. They saw their activities and called them the above names. Look how the book of Jude described him.

And the angels which kept not their first estate, but left their own habitation, he hath reserved in everlasting chains under darkness unto the judgment of the great day. - **Jude 6**

Likewise also these filthy dreamers defile the flesh, despise dominion, and speak evil of dignities. - **Jude 8**

Jude saw him as group of evil fallen angels, which kept not their first original estate; houses built for them by God. They left their own place of habitation, invaded the garden, and deceived Eve. They are responsible for filthy dreams that defile the body, pollute, and reduce human character to demonic character.

And the LORD God caused a deep sleep to fall upon Adam, and he slept: and he took one of his ribs, and closed up the flesh instead thereof; And the rib, which the LORD God had taken from man, made he a woman, and brought her unto the man. And Adam said, this is now bone of my bones, and flesh of my flesh: she shall be called Woman, because she was taken out of Man. Therefore shall a man leave his father and his mother, and shall cleave unto his wife: and they shall be one flesh. – **Genesis 2:21-24**

These dreams defile the original flesh God breathed in man; God's image and resemblance. Their aim is to destroy God's nature of righteousness breathed in man in the day of creation. They intend to destroy God's character in man, cause him to have the breath of the devil, character and image. They want to waste divine investment and install the devil's own image, desires and ways of life. His claim is that he married all women, and deceived all men in the day Eve disobeyed God. He does not respect any other marriage or recognize your person on earth. He enters into every throne and places of all the nations on earth without regarding your position. With all his royal demons that left heaven, they enter into places without respecting the security agent, keys and locked-up doors and gates. They despise dominions, authorities, and they even speak evil of dignities. They dehumanize kings, queens and princes on the thrones how much less people under them.

Thou shalt betroth a wife, and another man shall lie with her: thou shalt build an house, and thou shalt not dwell therein: thou shalt plant a vineyard, and shalt not gather the grapes thereof.
– Deuteronomy 28:30

You may physically sleep in your rented house or the house you built, but they can move you away spiritually from the house. In the dream, they can remove your clothes and put on you your high school uniform. They can bring you in your dreams to write an exam you wrote years ago and passed. They can take you to an office to work while you are still asleep in your house, right on top of your bed. They can force you to drive around, wonder about, walk about in strange places, eat in your dream, drink in the dream, have sex in your dreams, become pregnant in the dream, and give birth to spiritual children in your dreams.

If you ignore the above evil dreams activities, refuse to do something and wave it by your side, it may cause a lot of damage in your life physically and worse, spiritually. It can prevent you from getting married physically here on earth. It can delay your marriage, and if you marry at all, you may marry wrongly; your enemy.

At other times, you may be having serious marital problems. They may make sure you do not enjoy your marriage; to live in hostility with your partner and disagree all the time. To some, they may not be allowed to conceive, give birth to children, and abort whenever they conceive or prevent them from having godly children. These evil forces make life unbearable to their victims and frustrate their efforts in life. If they allow victims to have children at all, they pollute them, defile or destroy them through evil dreams while they are still in their mothers' womb.

Thy sons and thy daughters shall be given unto another people, and thine eyes shall look, and fail with longing for them all the day long: and there shall be no might in thine hand…Thou shalt beget sons and daughters, but thou shalt not enjoy them; for they shall go into captivity. – **Deuteronomy 28:32, 41**

The reason why many laws that protect women and children against the scriptures are passed is because of the evil influence of these evil powers on our leaders. These evil angels and demons start planting in some people's life right from their first entry into their mothers' womb. They sleep with their victims and claim to contribute in their conceptions while they sleep or do wrong things. They cause problems between husband and wife; set them against each other to fight, disagree and starve each other of sex. They separate them at night to have the whole night for sex to enable them to plant through sex, feeding them in their dreams to control their actions during the day. By so doing, even after they settle, come together, relate and conceive, what they planted start working on the conceived child right from the womb.

They defile children in the womb, attack their organs, their mental storehouse, and pollute their character. They capture some children in the womb, defile their desires, capture their destiny, stars and take full control over their activities on earth. Sometimes their activities manifest physically with deformity, sickness, disease or strange behaviours in the children. Their purpose is to make sure that parents, communities, nations, and even God do not enjoy those children.

To some, the plantation, defilements in the dreams attack them with different kind of problems. To some, it is poverty, lack, sufferings, hardship, wastes, delays, all manner of destructions, just name them. It can be failures, poor finishing, business failures or problems that come like locust.

Thou shalt carry much seed out into the field, and shalt gather but little in; for the locust shall consume it. Thou shalt plant vineyards, and dress them, but shalt neither drink of the wine, nor gather the grapes; for the worms shall eat them. – **Deuteronomy 28:38-39**

In deliverance school, we call them spiritual armed robbers or demons that come with problems on suicide missions. They attack victims with problems that will end their lives to the grave yards, deny some of a place in heaven, and destroy them eternally. They make the children of their victims foolish to bring calamity upon their parents. They fill their women victims with the demons of contention against their helpers.

A foolish son is the calamity of his father: and the contentions of a wife are a continual dropping. –**Proverbs 19:13**

Such women are blinded to attack their husband even unto death, under serious manipulations. They will be so possessed by these evil powers and controlled to their destruction until they separate, divorce or kill their husbands physically or spiritually. Their character makes them unmarriageable, disobedient, stubborn, foolish, contentious, bitter, angry, lazy, and violent unto destruction.

It is better to dwell in a corner of the housetop, than with a brawling woman in a wide house. - **Proverbs 21:9**

It is better to dwell in the wilderness, than with a contentious and an angry woman. – **Proverbs 21:19**

Others are deceitful, overly sexually possessed with wrong people, or under-sexually possessed with their rightful partner, husbands. Others can flatter, confuse, and can even rape men physically. They can make a wise man foolish, fearful, confused and deluded unto death, or to be destroyed eternally. Others can bring a man and his business down. They can wound or kill strong men, and take them to hellfire. Some women under evil influences are snares, filled with deaths that can kill without mercy. To some extent, they go out of normal sexual desires into lesbianism (Proverbs 21:9, 19; 7:21-22, 27; Ecclesiastes 7:26-28; Nehemiah 13:26; Jeremiah 16:1-4; Romans 1:26-27).

14 ACTIONS OF UNLIBERATED WOMEN

- ✓ The first human evil action on earth came through a woman (Genesis 3:1-7).
- ✓ The first spiritual marriage ever came through an unliberated woman (Deuteronomy 28:30).
- ✓ The first contention, quarrel, family misunderstanding ever on earth came through women with demonic nature (Proverbs 19:13).
- ✓ The first divorce ever recorded was caused by character-failed women on earth (Proverbs 21:9, 13).
- ✓ The first seduction, sexual violence or rape recorded came from undelivered women (Proverbs 7:21).
- ✓ The first love charm released against humanity came from evil, unsaved women (Proverbs 7:22).

- ✓ The first domestic violence released against family unity came from un-liberated woman (Proverbs 7:26).

- ✓ Deaths from women are more painful than the ones that come from men (Ecclesiastes 7:26; Judges 16:21-31; 2 Samuel 20:16-22; 2 Kings 11:1; Judges 9:16-24; 5:24-31).

- ✓ They are more heartless, more wicked and unrighteous than men (Ecclesiastes 7:27-28).

- ✓ They destroy the best in man faster than men that can destroy (Nehemiah 13:26).

- ✓ They can deny men of sex, starve them, punish them, and abandon them for lesbianism; thereby forcing men into homosexual (Romans 1:26-27).

- ✓ Un-liberated women are filled with death demons, and are like refuse dumps, shitholes, dangerous weapons in the hands of the devil, famine, bad luck, and full of dead bodies (Jeremiah 16:1-4).

- ✓ They stand as open doors and free ways to deaths and hell (Proverbs 7:27).

- ✓ The build walls to block heaven and force their victims to enter hellfire (Exodus 4:24-26).

THE WOMAN THAT SITS UPON MANY WATERS

The promotion of women above men against the word of God, and women's usurpation of power above men in some cultures started when Eve bowed to the serpent in the Garden of Eden. The devil promoted women, and began to manifest as female spirit to attack people spiritually. This is the principality that attacked the first church, persecuted and killed many of them. This spirit demanded for the head of John the Baptist and got it. She entered spiritually into every government, people under the government, and demanded that Christ must be crucified. She killed all the Disciples of Christ except John. Later, she possessed Emperor Domitian, demanded that John the beloved must die for standing for Christ. The authority arrested John, insulted him with hope that he will deny Christ, but he refused. In their last meeting, they decided to boil him on fire. At the end of the ends, John survived by miracles. They decided to abandon him the prison; an isolated island called Patmos. While he was there, Christ appeared to him with seven angels. He was commanded to write what he saw and heard from them. In obedience, he wrote the Book of Revelation, chapters one to sixteen.

At that point, one of the seven angels caught his attention. He was invited spiritually in the spirits to see a particular throne. He was told that the woman behind all the suffering of believers of all ages and people on earth will not go free. She must be punished! There is a judgment attached to all her evil actions; wicked acts on earth. There were other evil powers on earth, but the scriptures described this woman as the great whore.

And there came one of the seven angels which had the seven vials, and talked with me, saying unto me, Come hither; I will shew unto thee the judgment of the great whore that sitteth upon many waters: With whom the kings of the earth have committed fornication, and the inhabitants of the earth have been made drunk with the wine of her fornication. So he carried me away in the spirit into the wilderness: and I saw a woman sit upon a scarlet coloured beast, full of names of blasphemy, having seven heads and ten horns. – **Revelation 17:1-3**

In the vision, John saw this woman sitting upon many waters. In addition, she was linked in covenant with the kings or the world leaders of the earth of every nation. She commits fornication or in covenant relationship with world powers; the leaders of every nation. Through the world leaders, she corrupts the people under them worldwide as an evil coordinator. She gives leaders evil traditions, customs and laws that will separate them from God in order to corrupt everyone under each leader. Rights, judgments or decrees like abortion, lesbianism, gay and other laws that contradict God's word are not from the leaders. They come from this woman. The leaders just obey her command to keep their position as presidents, governors, law makers, or to keep any level of position received from her kingdom. That is why most leaders join cults, witchcraft groups or practice evil consultation. Some presidents and law makers may not be gay, but they encourage others to be. It is an order given to them by this woman to keep their position and maintain relationship with her.

And the woman was arrayed in purple and scarlet colour, and decked with gold and precious stones and pearls, having a golden cup in her hand full of abominations and filthiness of her fornication: And upon her forehead was a name written, MYSTERY, BABYLON THE GREAT, THE MOTHER OF HARLOTS AND ABOMINATIONS OF THE EARTH. – **Revelation 17:4-5**

The beast is a Gentile world leader now, or an example of the world leader that will emerge in the future. The woman sitting upon the beast, government in power or the president is the present backslidden worldwide apostate church. They seem to be supporting the worldwide president in place now or that will come into power later. The backslidden church or the woman sitting upon the beast, controlling the president, praying for him, supporting him to take over the holy city of Jerusalem and rule the world will soon be judged as told John in Revelation.

The beast, world president, is in many cults with many names of those cults already in the church; having initiated many church leaders, general overseers, and powerful elders in the church. Many pastors and church members already have names that blasphemes God's names. The seven heads represents seven kingdoms, powerful nations; and the ten horns also talks of nations and their powers that are already supporting the beast or that will give their support.

The woman or the church in verse four has the world's wealth all around her; with gold and every good thing you can think of in this earth. The golden cup in her hand represents money, and anything that money can offer at every level of need. But before you can have access to those purple, scarlet colours, gold precious stones and pearls, you must promise to do something or be doing something very bad as a condition to maintain, service the covenant agreement, or your relationship with her.

World leaders and pastors who because they wish to perform fake miracles, gather multitudes, great congregation, build estates, build cathedrals, make money, perform magic with fake testimonies of people vomiting keys, lizards; or to drive the latest cars, enter into cult, and become famous are deceived with their members. Fake miracle workers who bewitched their members to sow seeds or who destroy their members and sow seeds of cars or anything to exchange their destinies and kill them physically later will not escape God's judgment. They kill their followers or inhabitants spiritually or physically.

Ministers who are filled with pride, boasting, greed, anger, immorality, jealousy, covetousness, evil desires, loving temporary things above spiritual blessings, prosperity without holiness, miracles workers without salvation or just one of the above are deceived. They are operating under the control of this evil woman and they are deceived. They operate under the counterfeit from the great whore that sits upon many waters (Exodus 7:10-13,

20-22; 8:5-7, 20-23; 1 Samuel 18:10, 11; Ezekiel 9:1-4; Revelation 13:11-17; 2 Thessalonians 2:7-12).

And I saw the woman drunken with the blood of the saints, and with the blood of the martyrs of Jesus: and when I saw her, I wondered with great admiration. And the angel said unto me, wherefore didst thou marvel? I will tell thee the mystery of the woman, and of the beast that carrieth her, which hath the seven heads and ten horns. – **Revelation 17:6-7**

All the empires many ministers are building in the name of cathedral are only good and acceptable if the people worshipping there have the life of Christ. Anything less than Christ-like life is building mystery Babylon. Many ministers have converted their ministries to evil gathering because of one evil relationship or compromise. A single evil doctrine, uncompromising evil character, or addiction can convert your ministry to an evil coven with members still praying in the name of Christ under the control of the mother of Harlots.

Do you know that there are many pastors who service their evil by boasting, pride, living immoral lifestyle and other abominable acts? Many pastors are drinking the blood of their members by keeping them in bondage of sickness, poverty, hardship, suffering, terrible fears and problems that comes and goes? It is easier to leave some cults groups today than to leave some churches now because of the fear of what will happen to them by leaving, even when God says leave. It is easier for some people to change accommodation, school, city, and nation or even to separate or divorce than to leave some particular so called men of God or their ministry. Many people are suffering, dying and smiling in many churches today because of occult ministers and their ministries. So many ministers and their ministries who used to be vibrant, godly and powerful have been taken over and converted to mystery Babylon, the mother of Harlots and a place of abomination. Many good Christians in their midst have ignorantly died in their midst and many are still suffering (Hosea 4:6; Colossians 2:8).

Many know that their pastors and their ministries are out of God's plan, but they remained and died in their problems. The blood of many living saints, truly born again Christians, is being drunk by their pastors' right inside many churches, but some powers are holding them down. Others are confused, wondering, saying or thinking, "If God is not with our pastor, how come all his prophesies come to pass? Why is he still healing the sick, casting out demons, performing miracles, gathering cloud and being blessed? Why are his enemies being cursed when he cursed them and everything he says come to pass? Why is he getting better and better every day why those who live holy suffer and are getting poorer and poorer, dying younger?"

The answer is simple. The woman that sits upon many waters is promoting them, blessing them with defiled blessings in exchange for their souls.

Then all the men which knew that their wives had burned incense unto other gods, and all the women that stood by, a great multitude, even all the people that dwelt in the land of Egypt, in Pathros, answered Jeremiah, saying, As for the word that thou hast spoken unto us in the name of the LORD, we will not hearken unto thee. But we will certainly do whatsoever thing goeth forth out of our own mouth, to burn incense unto the queen of heaven, and to pour out drink offerings unto her, as we have done, we, and our fathers, our kings, and our princes, in the cities of Judah, and in the streets of Jerusalem: for then had we plenty of victuals, and were well, and saw no evil. But since we left off to burn incense to the queen of heaven, and to pour out drink offerings unto her, we have wanted all things, and have been consumed by the sword and by the famine. – **Jeremiah 44:15-18**

The woman that sits upon many waters answers many names in many places to deceive her victims. In the days of Jeremiah, he deceived the children of Israel with a name called the queen of heaven, with a promise of prosperity as long as they remain committed to her. To avoid suffering, hardship, famine, wars, health, long life and want of all things, they decided to remain in wrong covenant against the word of God. Likewise, many pastors and their members know that what they are doing is wrong, but they are afraid of fighting poverty, problems, and other life challenges in the right way. They are not ready to wait for God's time. The worse is that they are drinking the blood, and wasting destinies of ignorant, innocent holy members, the saints.

They are sitting upon the marriages, health's, business, glories, future and the Promised Land of many good Christians in their midst. Run for your life! They confuse their members with what the scriptures call lying wonders, not miracle because they can never cast out demons. They transfer demons, problems, or suspend them from actions for a season and after it may start in another form. That is why their members keep having problems without rest because they depend on their pastors instead of God. The devil has so much advanced in evil and deceit, and can keep his agents in prosperity, good health and want of nothing good to destroy them later. He can allow his committed agents to buy on credit, but will pay with their life in eternity, forever and ever.

Not everyone that saith unto me, Lord, Lord, shall enter into the kingdom of heaven; but he that doeth the will of my Father which is in heaven. Many will say to me in that day, Lord, Lord, have we not prophesied in thy name? and in thy name have cast out devils? and in thy name done many wonderful works? And then will I profess unto them, I never knew you: depart from me, ye that work iniquity. –**Matthew 7:21-23**

To some deceived people, the devil can allow you, assist you, empower you to sing like an angel, preach like Christ, have the knowledge of the bible, and recite the whole bible off hand as long as he hold you with one uncompromising sin. To some others, you can gather the whole city, move the crowd with wonderful entertainments, great prophetic utterances, anointing, and yet will not allow you to live holy which is the main purpose of Christianity and the essence of ministry. Once he is sure that Christ will tell you to depart from him on the last days, he can give you whatever you want. You just need to put your hand into the golden cup and pick one abomination and the filthy things you will be doing secretly to service the covenant to keep your relationship or fornication with the woman. Prosperity may keep coming.

If you are a pastor or an elder, and you prefer to do your own abomination in the church, no problems. She can allow you. If you want power, health, a child, prosperity at all cost, you do not want to wait for God, no problems. She can empower you right inside the church.

Then the devil taketh him up into the holy city, and setteth him on a pinnacle of the temple - **Matthew 4:5**

And saith unto him, All these things will I give thee, if thou wilt fall down and worship me. – **Matthew 4:9**

Once you can fall down any place and worship the devil, may be just once, you can be empowered to buy cars, distribute cars, build houses, control wealth and build estates. It may be just one time relationship, just few confessions hoping that you will repent later. You are deceived! Some ministers have given the devil the first position in their life and ministry, and come back to run ministry and they are prospering. But let me tell you the truth. You cannot mock God, compel him, or force him to take the second position in your life and ministry. No matter how much charity or miracles going on in your ministry, it is a deceit. God expects more than eighty percent of the present ministers to humble themselves, pack up their ministries, and join first timers' class in another ministry. It seems difficult and impossible, but that is the condition if you do not want to hear, depart from me, ye that work iniquity. It sound foolish but it is truth. God is a jealous God and cannot take second place or change because of you. Moreover, the devil has advanced in evil; changed his tactics and decided not to take immediate action against ministers and leaders working for him.

Finally, this is the last days, the end time (Psalms 74:4, 7-9), the devil has changed his system by assisting his followers to prosper while he attacks true believers, and God allows it to know where their faith lies. Remember, that was what happened in the days of Zacharias, Elizabeth, Simeon and Virgin Mary. Do not give up because the judgment is about to start against the evil powers fighting you. Even John in the last day, hours of his trials, when God was about to reward him of all his labors on earth almost compromised and started admiring the woman that sits upon many waters. He almost backslid, but God's angel intervened.

And I saw the woman drunken with the blood of the saints, and with the blood of the martyrs of Jesus: and when I saw her, I wondered with great admiration. And the angel said unto me, wherefore didst thou marvel? I will tell thee the mystery of the woman, and of the beast that carrieth her, which hath the seven heads and ten horns… And he saith unto me, the waters which thou sawest, where the whore sitteth, are peoples, and multitudes, and nations, and tongues. – **Revelation 17:6-7, 15**

The angel stopped him and gave him the mystery behind the prosperity of sinners; the mystery behind the evil wealth among the unrighteous ones in and outside the church; the reasons for the wealth of the cultists and the people in authority. He stopped John and told him the mystery behind all the ministers building big cathedrals without God in them and the life of Christ in the members. He told him the mystery of the woman that is blessing sinners in the church and attacking true worshippers. He told him that the waters he saw where the woman is sitting in verse one of the Book of Revelation 17, explained in verse fifteen are not ordinary waters.

They are people's destinies, glories, marriages and everything God destined for them to enjoy in life. They are people's finances, health and everything good made available for them by God, but this evil woman is sitting upon them. She sized them, only distributing them to people who commit fornication with her by covenants. He explained to John, just as you are being explained to today, and asked John not to admire her wealth, beauties, enjoyments, blessings and anything she can offer. The angel encouraged John to be patient, keep believing God for provision, and wait for his time in life or at death.

The mystery of the beast that is caring her in verse three of Revelation 17 is the beast that will break the covenant with Israel during the great tribulation. The world powers are gathering into two groups now and some are supporting America while the others are on the other side. After disagreement, they will eventually unite and form one union. One among them will be allowed to lead and he will break covenant with Israel and the woman, which is the backslidden church, the mystery Babylon; left behind during rapture will try to play along but will be rejected.

These have one mind, and shall give their power and strength unto the beast. These shall make war with the Lamb, and the Lamb shall overcome them: for he is Lord of lords, and King of kings: and they that are with him are called, and chosen, and faithful. And he saith unto me, the waters which thou sawest, where the whore sitteth, are peoples, and multitudes, and nations, and tongues. And the ten horns which thou sawest upon the beast, these shall hate the whore, and shall make her desolate and naked, and shall eat her flesh, and burn her with fire. For God hath put in their hearts to fulfil his will, and to agree, and give their kingdom unto the beast, until the words of God shall be fulfilled. And the woman which thou sawest is that great city, which reigneth over the kings of the earth. – **Revelation 17:13-18**

That leader is possibly America, or whichever country will come after Israel, the backslidden church and the tribulation saints. The devil will leave the bottomless pit, enter into the world president known as the beast, and with one mind of all other world leaders to destroy Israel. But as usual, God will intervene (Jeremiah 30:7). It will be a great day as never before in the history of the world, called the time of Jacobs's trouble but God will save Israel.

QUALITIES OF OVERCOMERS AMONG WOMEN

After the rapture, the remaining ones on earth will suffer greatly, especially women and the children. Today, God is searching for the women he will use to save the rest of the world. He wants to use you to deliver people from the activities of the beast during the last days, the days of antichrist. God is looking for responsibly women, who are liable, trustworthy women with the ability to discern right and wrong; women that will stand for the truth against wrongs and do the right things in the midst of oppositions.

God wants to give women the last opportunity to do what Eve could not do; a specific assignment, an office, duty or trust to disgrace the powers of darkness. He wants to empower women, develop them, help them, and use them to do what no one has done since the world began in this end time. He wants to prepare such women to prepare others for the rapture. He is searching for women who are purposeful, excellent and Christ-like in behaviour. God has no limit to what he can do with any woman who will cooperate this time with him. Therefore, God wants to put the marks of virtuousness in you, no matter how dirty, unworthy and sinful you may have been. What he demands is your readiness to change, repent, acknowledge your sins, confess and ask for power to sin no more.

Are you ready? If you are ready, God will transform you and make you:

1. Submissive as Sarah (1 Peter 3:4-6).
2. To be filled with gracious words as Abigail.
3. To be totally yielded as Ruth.
4. To be as chaste as Virgin Mary.
5. To be as hardworking and charitable as Dorcas.
6. To be stable in character.
7. To inspire and give confidence to others.
8. To be wise, tactful and discreet in management.
9. To be foresighted and un-wasteful.
10. To discover yourself, office and scope of assignment.

11. To be busy, not merely reclined on a chair, dishing out orders but will personally be engaged in daily chores.

12. To know and have correct use of your tongue.

13. To be holy, purposeful and principled in life.

14. To be modelled like Esther (Esther 2:7-10, 17; 4:15-16; 5:1-4; 7:1-6).

15. To patiently wait and be industrious like the Shunemite woman (2 Kings 4:8-10).

16. To remain holy like Elizabeth (Luke 1:5-7, 23-25, 57-64).

17. To remain undefiled like Virgin Mary (Luke 2:19; Matthew 2:13, 14, 19-22; Luke 2:41-48).

18. To be like the Hebrews midwives (Exodus 2:1-10).

19. To sing in holiness like Miriam, confront matters like the daughters of Zelophehad (Numbers 27:1-11; Joshua 17:3-6. Exodus 15:20-21).

20. To act like Rehab, Joel and Deborah (Joshua 2:1-24; Judges 9:18-24; 5:1-31).

21. To be like Manoah's wife, Ruth and Hannah (Judges 13:1-25; 14:1-3; Ruth 1:6-22; 2:2-3; 1 Samuel 1:5-6, 9-28).

22. To be as wise as Abigail, the widow of Zerephath, wife of one of the sons of the prophets (1Samuel 25:18-25; 1 Kings 17:8-16; 2 Kings 4:1-7).

23. To preach like the little maid, a woman, the woman of Canaan and the wife of the Pilate (2 Kings 5:1-7; 2 Kings 8:1-6; Matthew 15:21-37; 27:19).

24. To support like Mary Magdalene (Matthew 28:1-2, 5-10; Mark 15:39-41, 47; 16:1-10, 19, 20; Luke 23:47-49, 55-56; 24:1-12).

25. To advertise like the woman of Samaria, Phebe and Dorcas (John 4:28-30; Romans 16:1-2. Acts 9:36-43).

26. To be faithful and determined like the woman of the issue of blood (Luke 8:43-48; 13:11-13).

27. Like other women who were tender in heart and with forgiving spirit (Ephesians 4:32; Colossians 3:12-14).

28. Like women who did not give the devil any chance to act or have a place (Ephesians 4:27; Luke 11:24-26; 1 Peter 5:8-9; James 4:7).

29. Women of secret prayer life (Luke 18:1; Acts 6:4; 2 Corinthians 10:4-5).

30. Women of holiness, inner victory and freedom (Hebrews 4:9; Ephesians 5:26-27; John 8:36).

Others qualities include being women of like minds, who practice self-denial (Matthew 16:24-25; Hebrews 11:24-27; Exodus 32:10-14; Philippians 3:7-8; Romans 15:2-3). God is also searching for women of simplicity and sincerity (Mark 10:39-42; 25:31-46; John 13:4-6; Romans 12:8-9). He is also, searching for women of succour and supply (2 Samuel 8:5; 21:15-17; 2 Corinthians 8:14). More women in the list of God's search are women who are serious and sensitive (John 13:4-5; 1 Peter 4:8-10; James 5:16; 1 Peter 1:22). More women in the list are women their words can edify and minister grace to the ears of their hearers (Ephesians 4:29; Colossians 4:6). Included among these are women of sound principles, industry and labors (1

Samuel 12:3-5; Romans 12:17; 1 Corinthians 8:21; Ephesians 4:28; Acts 20:35).

38 CHARACTERISTICS OF UNMARRIAGEABLE WOMEN

There are characteristics peculiar to evil women, unliberated women, unmarriageable women who are deceived by the devil and water spirit in all generations. Evil women in covenant with water spirit break God's covenant. Below are their manifestations:

1. They are possessed with strange behavior **(Prov. 2:16)**.

2. They have plastering lips **(Proverbs 2: 16)**.

3. They easily forsake good training **(Proverbs 2: 17)**.

4. They abandon God's covenant too fast **(Proverbs 2: 17)**.

5. At the hours of deceit, they use sweet tongues **(Pro. 5:13)**.

6. When scheming to draw people to themselves for destruction, they may speak softly at times.

7. During attack of their victims, they are easily destructive **(Prov. 5:4)**.

8. In terms of relationship, they are like chameleon, moveable and unreliable in character **(Prov. 5:6)**.

9. Evil women possess mixed character; at times, they are extremely clever, lazy, dullards or very brilliant (intelligent) **(Proverbs 5:6)**.

10. In response to God's demands, they are stubbornly disobedient or sluggish **(Proverbs 9 – 11)**.

11. They possess proud looking dispositions **(Proverbs 6:17)**.

12. They have sharp lying tongues **(Proverbs 6:17)**.

13. Their hands shed innocent blood **(Proverbs 6:17)**.

14. They indulge in wicked imagination because they possess defiled hearts **(Proverbs 6:18)**.

15. They are very fast at times, clever and masterful in doing evil **(Proverbs 6:18)**.

16. They bear false witness and tell unsuspecting lies **(Proverbs 6: 19)**.

17. They sow the seed of discord among brethren **(Proverbs 6:19)**.

18. They entangle people in their words **(Proverbs 7: 5)**.

19. They are very subtle and most of them dress in a nude way to destroy **(Proverbs 7:10)**.

20. They are very stubborn and loud **(Proverbs 7:11)**.

21. They have the anointing of walker about, vagabond spirit, inconsistent lifestyle **(Proverbs 7: 11-12)**.

22. They are possessed with fake love, which they distribute from person to person for the purpose of destruction **(Proverbs 7: 13-23)**.

23. Their behavior and actions induce people into all manner of evil **(Proverbs 7: 3-23)**.

24. At times, their speech is soft but in the end, destructive **(Proverbs 7: 13-23)**.

25. They are champions in persuading people to do evil **(Proverbs 7: 13-23)**.

26. Their speech is continually, persistent to do evil things **(Proverbs 7: 21-23)**.

27. The have the evil ability to control men **(Proverbs 7: 21-22)**.

28. They distribute incurable sickness and diseases **(Proverbs 7:23)**.

29. They set traps and put ignorant people into them **(Proverbs 7:26)**.

30. They wound people's great destinies **(Proverbs 7:26)**.

31. They kill great destined people in all generation **(Proverbs 7:26)**.

32. The drag people down to the chambers of death and hell **(Proverbs 7:27)**.

33. They are very contentious and ceaseless in abusive language **(Proverbs 19:13)**.

34. They are very brawling in nature **(Proverbs 21:9,25:24)**

35. Their words trap simple minded backsliders and sinners **(Proverbs 22:14)**.

36. They are evil determined personalities **(Proverbs 27:15)**.

37. Confidence in them is like wind that blows across **(Proverbs 27:16)**.

38. They are very cunning and clever like their mother, the queen of heaven **(Proverbs 30:20)**.

The agents of the water spirit break God's covenant with joy. They are very deceitful and wicked. They start relationships with fake humility but full of lies. The end of evil relationships with evil women in covenant with the water spirits brings death. The only solution is repentance and perfect separation **(Proverbs 5: 3-4)**. They destroy their own marriage with their own hands. One of the greatest mistakes of any true believer is to get married to them. John Wesley was a great minister. He was a real man of God who preached and evangelized effectively. He built up the early Methodist Church. He improvingly built up many lives. He wrote commentaries on the whole

Bible, preached and wrote many life-changing sermons. Yet he made mistake in choosing a wife. We had better listen to those who have tasted all the things which we are pursuing today. I am talking about those who have examined the present from the past: from the beginning to the end. One of such people is Solomon, the son of David.

27 CHARACTERISTICS OF GOOD WOMEN

1. **Godly** women do everything good possible to retain their honor **(Prov. 11:16)**.

2. They love and protect their husbands **(Prov. 12:4; 31:23)**.

3. They are not abusive, especially to their husbands **(Prov. 12:25)**

4. They openly; commend their husbands and secretly rebuke them with respect **(Prov. 27:5; 28:23)**.

5. They don't think evil against their husbands **(Prov. 31: 10-12)**.

6. They are industrious **(Prov. 13:13)**.

7. They hate laziness **(Prov. 31:13)**.

8. Good women are not idle people **(Prov. 31:14)**.

9. Good women give adequate support to their family **(Prov. 31:14)**.

10. They are not discriminative or selective in caring in their house **(Prov. 31:15)**.

11. Good women engage themselves profitably **(Prov. 31:16)**.

12. They are courageous and do not exhibit cowardice **(Prov. 31:7)**.

13. They are always in the spirit **(Prov. 31:17)**.

14. They are heavenly minded and they do everything with eternity in view **(Prov. 31:18)**.

15. Hardship does not intimidate them **(Prov. 31:90)**.

16. They show compassion on people **(Prov. 31:20)**.

17. They are fearless and bold like a lion **(Prov. 31:21)**.

18. They provide for themselves and others **(Prov. 31:20, 22)**.

19. They possess new breakthrough skills **(Prov. 31:24)**.

20. Their works are perfect **(Prov. 31:25)**.

21. Their speech is reasonably spoken in wisdom and in season **(Prov. 31:26)**.

22. Their words are full of kindness **(Prov. 31:26)**.

23. They are not parasites, burden to others **(Prov. 31:27)**.

24. They guide their children into good training **(Prov. 31:18)**.

25. Their works are done excellently **(Prov. 31:29)**.

26. They fear only but God **(Prov. 31:30)**.

27. Their work praises them **(Prov. 31:31)**.

THE RAPTURE OF THE SAINTS

HOW IT WILL HAPPEN

Just as Elijah, Enoch, and Noah were taken away to safety in the times of troubles so also the saints, true believers who are born again, living a holy life at the moment of rapture or death will be translated to meet the Lord in the air.

You remember that at the time of flood, Noah escaped and Lot escaped the judgment of fire on Sodom and Gomorrah. That is how the saints will be raptured (1 Thessalonians 4:13-18; John 14:1-3; 1 Corinthians 15:23, 51-58; Luke 21:34-36).

THE TRUTH ABOUT THE RAPTURE

All the prophecies that must be fulfilled before the rapture takes place are being fulfilled right before us now - Matthew 24:37-39; 1 Timothy 4:1-3; 2 Timothy 3:1-5; Acts 2:17-18; 3:20-21; 2 Peter 3:3-4.

If you are not ready for the rapture now, you are deceived and you have put yourself in danger of troubles that is about to start - Jeremiah 30:7.

Rapture means the catching up of all truly born again Christians to meet the Lord in the air.

It is a time when Christ comes for the saints.

At rapture, Christ does not appear visibly to those on the earth. He only appears in the air to resurrect the true saints who have died, change the living saints and catch them up to meet the Lord in the air.

It will take place in a moment of time, in the twinkling of an eye – 1 Corinthians 15:23, 51-58; Philippians 3:20-21; 1 Thessalonians 4:13-17.

We shall be changed and caught up; transformed and translated - Genesis 5:24; Hebrews 11:5; 2 Kings 2:11-12; Acts 1:9-11.

THE REASON FOR THE RAPTURE

To raise the saints who have died (1 Thessalonians 4:13-16; 1 Corinthians 15:21-23, 51-58; Revelation 20:4-6).

To transform the bodies of living saints who are holy at that moment from mortality to immortality (1 Corinthians 15:51-58; Philippians 3:20-21; 2 Corinthians 5:1-8).

To remove all the saints out of this world before the great tribulation (1 Thessalonians 4:13-17; Luke 21:34-36; 2 Thessalonians 2:1, 7-8; Genesis 19:12-17).

To take the saints as His inheritance (John 14:1-3; 1 Thessalonians 4:17; Ephesians 5:27; 2 Thessalonians 2:1).

To bring all the saints together for the marriage supper of the lamb and give them rewards for their work (Revelation 19:1-11; 2 Corinthians 5:8-10).

QUALIFICATION TO BE RAPTURED

To be raptured, you have to maintain a holy walk with Christ all the time, especially at the time of rapture.

To be raptured, you have to be holy and maintain good relationship with God at the time of death - Amos 4:12.

To be raptured, you have to be steadfast, unmovable, and working for God - 1 Corinthians 15:58; Revelation 2:26; 3:11.

Rapture is different from the Second Advent or second coming of Christ - Zacharias 14:1-5; Jude14; Revelation 19:11-21.

Second coming is the time Christ comes to the earth with the saints. The rapture can take place any moment, any time from now because we are living in the last days of this age. If you are not ready to meet the Lord now, you are in a fearful position and in a terrible mess.

THE JUDGMENT SEAT OF GOD OR BEMA

(2 Corinthians 5:1-10; Romans 14:10-12; 1 Corinthians 3:6-15; Revelation 19:7-8)

THE JUDGMENT EXPLAINED

Immediately after the rapture, two programs will take place at the same time. The first one is referred to as appearing before the judgment seat of Christ. This judgment is for believers and it is not a time to consider his salvation or question it. Every sinful question is settled before rapture - Romans 8:1; John 5:24; 1 John 4:17.

The purpose of this judgment is to examine believers work and know how to reward each one - 2 Corinthians 5:1-10.

After the *bema* judgment and reward receiving, there will be marriage with Christ, called the *Marriage Supper of the Lamb* - Revelation 19:7-8.

The meaning of judgment seat of Christ explained in: 2 Corinthians 5:10; Romans 14:10.

The Greek word is "**bema**" translated judgment seat; meaning; reward seat.

The time of the bema judgment of Christ - Luke 14:12-14; 1 Corinthians 4:5; 2 Timothy 4:8; Revelation 22:12.

The place the judgment reward will take place is in the air, heavenly place, in the presence of God - 1 Thessalonians 4:17; 2 Corinthians 5:1-8.

Jesus Christ is going to be the judge during the bema reward.

(2 Corinthians 5:10; John 5:22; Romans 14:10; Revelation 2:7, 17, 25-28; 3:12, 21; 22:12-16)

He will give believers rewards according to their works.

Every believers work shall be tested by fire - 1 Corinthians 3:8-15.

Some shall suffer loss, which is loss of rewards; others will receive reward 1 Corinthians 3:13-15.

TYPES OF REWARDS

The soul winner's reward is crown of rejoicing - 1 Thessalonians 2:19; Daniel 12:3.

The overcomers' reward is incorruptible crown - 1 Corinthians 9:25.

The crown of life, for tested, tried, and triumphant saints - James 1:12.

The crown of glory, for feeding the flock of God - 1 Peter 5:4.

The crown of righteousness, for loving His appearance - 2 Timothy 4:8.

The kind of rewards you receive determines where you will seat before the marriage commences.

THE PROPER MARRIGE

(THE MARRIAGE OF THE LAMB)

(JOHN 3:29; ROMANS 7:4; 2 CORINTHIANS 11:2; EPHESIANS 5:25-33; REVELATION 19:7, 8; 21:1-22)

This marriage will bring the true church, the raptured saints, all believers into an eternal union with Christ. It will take place between the *bema* rewards and the second advent of Christ.

Jesus Christ is the bridegroom - Revelation 19:7; Matthew 9:14-15; John 3:27-30; 2 Corinthians 11:2; Ephesians 5:25-27, 32.

The bride of the Lamb - Revelation 19:7-8; 2 Corinthians 11:2; Ephesians 5:25-27, 30-32.

The church will be the bride because the church is the chaste virgin, presented to Christ while Israel will be restored - 2 Corinthians 11:2.

The dress of the Bride is Righteousness - Revelation 19:8; Ephesians 5:25-27; 2 Corinthians 11:2.

Who are the blessed guests of the Lamb? - Revelation 19:9-10; John 3:28-29; Luke 13:28-29.

The saints of the Old Testament, believers, martyred during the Tribulation, end time redeemed Israel, and Gentiles apart from the church form the invited guests - Revelation 6:9-11.

GREAT TRIBULATION

General tribulation is the common problem that everyone on earth goes through [John 15:18-21; 16:33; Matthew 13:20, 21; Acts 14:21, 22; Romans 5:1-5; 8:35-39; 12:12; 2 Corinthians 1:3, 4; 7:4; Ephesians 3:12, 13; 1 Thessalonians 3:1-4; Revelation 1:9; 2:9].

Great Tribulation will occur after the rapture, and will take time at the same time with the *bema* judgment in different places.

During this time, the Antichrist will take possession of this world for the reign of terror.

He will be a system or organization, but also a person; a supernatural, diabolical being in the form of a man who will blaspheme and proclaim himself to be God - Daniel 8:23-25; 2 Thessalonians 2:7-12; Revelation 13:1-18; Jeremiah 30:5-7, 11-11; Daniel 9:27; 12:1; Matthew 24:3-38.

THE NATURE OF GREAT TRIBULATION

It will be a time of Trouble - Jeremiah 30:7; Zephaniah 1:14, 15; Daniel 12:1.

It will be a time of wrath - Zephaniah 1:15, 18; 1 Thessalonians 1:10; 5:9; Revelation 6:16, 17. 11:18; 14:10, 19; 15:1, 7; 16:1, 19.

It will be a time of judgment - Revelation 14:7; 15:4; 16:5, 7; 19:2.

It will be a time of trial - Revelation 3:10.

It will be a time of desolation - Daniel 9:27; Zephaniah 1:14, 15.

It will be a time of indignation - Isaiah 26:20, 21; 34:13.

It will be a time of overturning - Isaiah 24:1-4, 19-21.

It will be a time of punishment - Isaiah 24:20, 21.

THE PURPOSE OF THE GREAT TRIBULATION

Lack of the knowledge of the Scriptures makes people think that God cannot get angry against sin and sinners [2 Chronicles 28:10, 11; Job 21:14-20, 30; Psalms 106:21-29; 90:7-12; Isaiah 3:6-11; Nahum 1:2-8; Luke 3:7; Romans 2:3-9; Hebrews 2:3; 10:30, 31; 12:29; 5:24; Romans 8:1, 33-34; 1 Thessalonians 5:9].

TH PURPOSE ARE

The vengeance of God - Deuteronomy 32:35; Romans 12:19.

To prepare the nation Israel for her Messiah Christ - Deuteronomy 4:30, 31; Jeremiah 30:7; Ezekiel 20:37, 38; Daniel 12:1; Zechariah 13:8, 9.

To pour out judgment on sinful men in all nations - Revelation 3:10; Isaiah 26:20, 21; Jeremiah 25:30-33; 2 Thessalonians 2:8-12; Revelation 6:12-17; 16:8, 9.

The nature of God and the Word of God proves that God will punish sinners who refuse to repent because His unchanging Word declares so and Scriptures cannot be broken (Revelation 15:3, 4; Matthew 5:18).

THE SOURCE OF THE GREAT TRIBULATION

God is the source of the great tribulation because His wrath and judgment will fall upon the earth. Those who refuse to accept salvation must be forced to accept the wrath of the Lord (Isaiah 24:1; 26:21; Joel 1:15; Zephaniah 1:18; Revelation 6:16-17; 11:18; 14:7-8, 19; 15:4, 7; 16:1, 7, 19).

The tribulation period will be a terrible time as God's wrath will be poured out against all evil and evil doers - Revelation 6:15, 17; 16:5-6.

In addition, the devil and the Antichrist will release their wraths against sinners on earth. The devil comes down, having great wrath against all that is good and all inhabitants of the earth - Revelation 12:9, 12.

HOW LONG WILL GREAT TRIBULATION LAST?

(DANIEL 9:24-27; 2 THESSALONIANS 2:1-12; MATTHEW 24:15-22; MARK 13:14-20; REVELATION 11:2, 3; 12:6, 14; 13:5)

Great tribulation will last for 7 years which is called Daniel's seventeenth week. The world has spent the sixth week of the history and the only thing delaying the last seventh week is the rapture. In Daniel's prophesy, a week means seven, referring to seven years (Daniel 9:27). The last half of the week, that is the last half of the seven years, 3 1/2 years, 42 months or 1260 days, will be very disastrous because of the wrath of the Antichrist who will break his agreement with Israel in the midst of the week (Daniel 9:27).

EXPOSING ANTICHRIST, THE BEAST

John spoke of Antichrist in his epistle to believers. 1 John 2:18.

Even in the Old Testament, it was common knowledge from the Old Testament that Antichrist shall come. Daniel 7:8, 25. 8:23-25. 9:26, 27. 11:36-45. John 5:43. 2 Thessalonians 2:1-10.

Antichrist is anti-God, working against God's plan. In times of his reign on earth, during the great tribulation, he will fight against the truth; blaspheme God and war against the saints of the tribulation period. This diabolical personality will blaspheme the name of God relentlessly and continuously and literally, will cause millions of tribulation saints to die violent and painful death Revelation 13:7, 15. 6:3-8. 8:8-11. 11:3-6, 13, 18.

ADVICE TO TRIBULATION SAINTS

(REVELATION 13:9, 10. 3:6; ISAIAH 33:1; MATTHEW 26:51, 52; REVELATION 14:12)

Whatever a man sows, he will reap, and those who live by the sword will die by sword. Judgment must definitely come on all the evil doers. God's counsel for the tribulation saints left behind on earth after the rapture is patience and faithfulness throughout the period.

ANTICHRIST, THE KING OF FIERCE COUNTENANCE

(DANIEL 8:23-27)

The scriptures exposed the works of Antichrist as an individual who will appear in the end time as the head of the Gentile power in their ten kingdom federation. His personality and works are presented in the following scriptures:

Ezekiel 28:1-10; Daniel 7:7-8, 20-26; 8:23-25; 9:26-27; 11:36-45; 2 Thessalonians2:3-10; Revelation 13:1-10; 17:8-14.

NAMES AND TITLES OF ANTICHRIST

- ✓ The little horn - Daniel 7:8.
- ✓ The king of fierce countenance - Daniel 8:21.
- ✓ The prince that shall come - Daniel 9:26.
- ✓ The desolator - Daniel 9:27.
- ✓ The vile person - Daniel 11:21.
- ✓ The wilful king - Daniel 11:36.
- ✓ The man of sin - Daniel 2; Thessalonians 2:3.
- ✓ The son of perdition - 2 Thessalonians 2:3.
- ✓ The lawless one - 2 Thessalonians 2:8.
- ✓ The Antichrist - 1 John 2:22.

REVELATIONAL FACTS CONCERNING ANTICHRIST'S ACTIVITIES

The Antichrist will be strong, vehement, a great intimidator, persecutor, and a demonic genius.

He will be mighty but not by his own power because he will be energized by Satan.

There will be a holocaust of devastation that is beyond description - Daniel 8:23-25.

His cunning is linked to deceit by treachery, by which he will accomplish his purpose.

Antichrist will be deceitful, treacherous, wise, brilliant, a satanically indwelt genius, and will gain control by lies and deceit.

The world will wonder at the power of his destruction.

He will appear on the stage in the last days of Israel's history - Daniel 8:23.

WHO IS HE, OR HINDERING HIM?

He will not fully manifest until the day of the Lord has begun - 2 Thessalonians 2:2.

His appearance is being delayed by the restrainer - 2 Thessalonians 2:6, 7.

His manifestation will be preceded by a departure from the faith or the rapture - 2 Thessalonians 2:3, 1.

He is a worldwide leader since he comes out from the sea - Revelation13:1; 17:15. Sea represents the Gentile nations, so he must be of Gentile origin.

He rises from the heathen nation, an empire, since he is a ruler of the people who will destroy Jerusalem - Daniel 9:26.

Antichrist is the head of the last form of Gentile world dominion, for he is like a Leopard, a bear, and a lion - Revelation 13:11; Daniel 7:7-8, 20, 24; 17:9-11.

Being a political leader, the seven heads and ten horns are federated under his authority - Revelation 13:1. 17:12.

He will have worldwide influence because he will rule the world and his influence will come through the alliance which he gained by cooperating with many nations - Daniel 8:24; Revelation 17:12.

Three main nations and their leaders that will oppose him at his rise to power will be eliminated. One of the kingdoms over which he will exercise authority will be revived or healed - Daniel 7:8, 24; Revelation 17:10; 13:3.

In order to win many in many nations and rise to power and prominence, he will come up with a peace program to deceive many - Daniel 8:25.

His personality will be marked by his subtlety, craft, and intelligent persuasions to many for evil, so that as you yield, you will not have anybody to blame - Daniel 7:8, 20; 8:23; Ezekiel 28:6; Revelation 17:13.

As he deceived the world into covenants and rules them in his federation with absolute authority, he will rule them according to his will. He will change law and customs to suit him Daniel 11:36; 7:25.

His major interest is might and power - Daniel 11:38.

As the head or leaders of federated empire, he entered into a seven-year covenant with Israel, which will be broke after three and one half years - Daniel 9:27.

He will promote idolatrous worships, assume the position of gods, and will receive worships - Daniel 9:27; 11:36-37; 2 Thessalonians 2:4; Revelation 13:5.

As he promotes himself as a deity, he begins to blaspheme God - Ezekiel 28:2; Daniel 7:25; Revelation 13:1, 5-6.

He will be empowered by Satan, acts in the authority of Satan who will fully begin to control him with his pride - Ezekiel 28:2; Daniel 8:25.

Satan will control him and use him to bring lawless system on earth. He will also be performing fake miracles and lying wonders through satanic powers - 2 Thessalonians 2:9-19; Psalm 74:1-11.

Because of the blindness of the deceived ones, he will rule as if he is God - 2 Thessalonians 2:11.

He will turn against the children of Israel as a worse adversary ever - Daniel 7:21, 25; 8:24; Revelation 13:7.

An alliance will come against him and contest his authority - Ezekiel 28:7; Daniel 11:40, 42.

The conflict will lead him to gain control over Palestine and adjacent boundaries and he will make Jerusalem his headquarters - Daniel 11:42.

He will be elevated through the instrumentality of the harlot, the corrupt religious system that may seek to dominate him - Revelation 17:3.

This corrupt system will later be destroyed by the antichrist to enable him rule without hindrance - Revelation 17:16, 17.

This will promote him to double his adversary against the Prince of Princes, His program and His people - Daniel 8:25; 2 Thessalonians 2:4; Revelation 17:14.

His power, reign, and every activity are only confined to the last three and half years of the tribulation period - Daniel 7:25; 9:27; 11:36; Revelation 13:5.

His leadership will be terminated by a direct judgment from God - Ezekiel 28:6; Daniel 7:22, 26; 8:25; 9:27; 11:45; Revelation 19:19-20.

The termination of his reign will occur as he is energized and engaged in a military campaign in Palestine - Ezekiel 28:8, 9; Revelation 19:19.

He will be cast into the lake of fire - Revelation 19:19; Ezekiel 28:10.

Immediately he is judged, the second advent of Christ will take place - 2 Thessalonians 2:8; Daniel 7:22.

This will give way to the Messianic reign and Christ's authority on earth - Revelation 11:15; Daniel 7:27.

THE SECOND COMING (ADVENT) OF CHRIST

(Matthew 24:29-35; Jude 14, 15; Revelation 1:7; 19:11-21)

Prophecy occupies one-fifth of scripture, and the second coming occupies one-third of that one-fifth. Of the 333 prophecies concerning Christ, only 109 of them were fulfilled in His first coming, leaving 224 yet to be fulfilled in His second coming. There are 7, 959 verses in the New Testament, 330 of which refer directly to the second coming. Jesus Christ, personally, refers to His return twenty-one times. Over fifty times, we are exhorted to be ready for the second coming of Jesus Christ.

The beginning of sorrow announced: Matthew 24:4-8; Revelation 6:1-17.

Antichrist's covenant with Israel: Matthew 24:9-26; Daniel 9:27; Revelation 6:1-17.

At the beginning of the seven years period of the Tribulation, Israel will enjoy peace under the false covenant (Daniel 9:27). In the middle of the evil relationship, the Antichrist will break the covenant (Matthew 24:9; Revelation 12:12-17). The Antichrist, which is also the desolator (Matthew 24:16-20), will be stopped by the second advent of Christ (Matthew 24:27-30).

THE BATTLE OF ARMAGEDDON

Immediately after the tribulation, Israel who were scattered will be gathered by special angelic ministry, the elect of Matthew 24:31 are referred to as Israel (Daniel 7:18-22, 27). The second coming will be glorious, wonderful, majestic, regal, and visible (Revelation 19:11-13; Zechariah 14:1-9; Isaiah 63:1-6; 64:1, 2; Matthew 24:29, 30).

At His first coming, He came like a baby, born by a woman, in humility to suffer, be insulted, to die and save the world.

At Christ's second coming, He will come in full power to conquer, judge, and reign.

He is coming as a warrior, faithful, true, chief justice and king of the world (Acts 17:31).

THE REIGN OF CHRIST AS WARRIOR AND CONQUEROR

(Revelation 19:14; Matthew 24:29-31; Jude 14, 15; Colossians 3:4)

Christ is coming to reign as a conqueror with angels and saints appearing with Him. Every raptured saint as warriors shall follow Him, putting on fine linens, clean and white, sitting upon white horses - Revelation 19:14; 2 Kings 2:11; 6:13-17.

THE DEVASTATION BY THE CONQUEROR

(Revelation 19:15, 16; Isaiah 11:4; Joel 3:13-16; Psalms 2:9)

Jesus will appear as KING of KINGS, AND LORD OF LORDS with divine majesty.

He is coming to rule and reign forever and ever.

He is coming with all power and glory to reign and rule the earth as King of kings and Lord of lords - Revelation 19:15-21; 20:1-4; Ezekiel 39:17-22.

In the battle of Armageddon, there will be a great and terrible slaughter on that day.

Satan and all sinners that will oppose Him will be destroyed by His mighty power - Revelation 14:19, 20; 17:14; 19:11-21; Isaiah 13:9; 29:57; 24:20.

The Antichrist will gather all sinners as his army from all nations of the earth to fight through the efforts of the evil spirits with his false prophets - Revelation 16:12-14.

This will be the last effort Satan will make to keep power, but he will fail woefully with the deceived world power he kept in sin under him.

THE RESURRECTION TO LIFE OR THE FIRST RESSURRECTION

FACTS ABOUT RESURRECTION

(HEBREWS 11:17, 18; JOB 19:25-27; PSALMS 49:15; DANIEL 12:2; ISAIAH 25:8; 26:19; JOHN 5:25, 28-29; JOHN 11:23-25; ACTS 24:15)

Both Old Testament and New Testament reveal the facts of the resurrection.

Between death and resurrection, sinners' souls were in Hell with consciousness.

They can see, hear, feel, and the same is applicable to a child of God who dies and goes to heaven (Luke 23:39-43; Acts 7:54-60; 2 Corinthians 5:1-8; Philippians 1:21-23; Luke 16:19-31).

When the time for resurrection comes, physical bodies are resurrected and souls from Heaven for the children of God; souls from Hell for the sinners are united with the resurrection bodies.

This part of resurrection program is called the resurrection of life, or the just; a better resurrection and the first resurrection.

It is a separation; a resurrection of a portion of those who are dead, but leaves some dead people, the unjust, in their graves for future resurrection.

EXAMPLES OF RESURRECTION

(1 CORINTHIANS 15:23)

Christ's resurrection from dead predicted (Matthew 16:21; 17:22-23; 20:17-19; Mark 8:31; 10:32-34; Luke 9:20-22; 18:31-34).

Christ's body described after resurrection (Luke 24:36-43; 24:31-36; John 20:11-20, 24-34).

His body was glorified after resurrection (1 Corinthians 15:35-38; 1 John 3:2; Matthew 22:30; 1 Corinthians 15:39-54).

Our bodies when resurrected like that of Christ will be immortalized, but will possess different degrees of glory.

THE RESURRECTION OF THE UNSAVED DEAD; SECOND OR DAMNATION

MORE FACTS ABOUT RESURRECTION

Centuries ago, Christ resurrected - 1 Corinthians 15:3-4, 12, 20, 23.

At rapture, the dead saints will be resurrected - 1 Thessalonians 4:13-16.

The saints who went through tribulation will be resurrected after 7 years - Revelation 20:3-15.

At the Second Advent, the Old Testament saints, will be resurrected - Daniel 12:2; Isaiah 26:19.

All the unsaved dead will be resurrected - Revelation 20:11-15; Job 14:12. This includes those whose bodies were destroyed or devoured by voracious fish into millions of small bits; they will be raised by the power of resurrection - Philippians 3:10; Romans 8:11.

SECOND, DAMNATION, OR RESURRECTION OF THE UNSAVED

(DANIEL 12:2; JOHN 5:28-29; REVELATION 20:4-5, 11-15)

Dead sinners of all the ages will also have bodily resurrection.

At that time, all creatures, including the sea and the graves will give up their dead.

This part of resurrection program deals with the unsaved.

People involved in this kind of resurrection will receive eternal judgment from the impartial Righteous Judge.

The resurrection is called the resurrection of the unjust, the unsaved, or the resurrection to shame and everlasting contempt.

It will take place after the millennium - one thousand years.

All the resurrected sinners will be punished in the lake of fire because their names are not found in the Book of Life.

THE MILLENNIAL REIGN OF CHRIST

LIFE ON EARTH WITHOUT SATAN

The millennial kingdom is the coming golden age when Christ rules in power on earth - Revelation 20:1-10.

It is going to be a reign of Christ for 1000 years on earth.

HOW WILL HIS REIGN BE WITHOUT SATAN'S ACTIVITIES ON EARTH FOR SUCH PERIOD?

- ✓ The period will be characterized by peace - Isaiah 2:2-5; 11:1-9; 54:13; Ezekiel 34:25, 28; Hosea 2:18; Micah 4:2-3; Zechariah 9:10.
- ✓ It will be a time dominated by happiness - Isaiah 12:1-6.
- ✓ It will be a period of time full of long life and divine health
- ✓ Isaiah 33:24; 65:18-20; Jeremiah 30:17; Ezekiel 34:16.
- ✓ The period will be filled with prosperity - Isaiah 35:1-10.

- ✓ There will be joy in every labor - Isaiah 65:21-25; 9:3-4.
- ✓ The survivors of the great tribulation will be having children but the saints will not - Isaiah 11:6-8; 65:20; 41:8-14; 62:8, 9; Jeremiah 32:27; Ezekiel 34:27.
- ✓ It will be a time of theocratic rule, which is a government of the state by the immediate direction of God.
- ✓ It will be a rule of God through a divinely chosen representatives who speaks and acts for the Almighty as directed by Christ.
- ✓ There will be a full manifestation of God's glory through Jesus Christ.
- ✓ It will be a time of the manifestation of the glorious universal dominion of Christ's absolute power - Isaiah 9:6; Psalms 45:4; Isaiah11:4; Psalms 72:4; 2:9.
- ✓ The judiciary department in which Christ is the spokesman for the Almighty God will be announcing God's will at all time - Isaiah 2:3-4; 33:21-22; Isaiah 42:4; Acts 3:22.

- ✓ Christ will seat on the throne as David's son to fulfil the promise to David (2 Samuel 7:12-16; Isaiah 9:6-7; Luke 1:31-33; Matthew 25:21).
- ✓ There will be divine mercy, goodness, and divine truth which will be released through Christ the King (Isaiah 40:10-13; 54:710; Jeremiah 33:9; Zechariah 3:10; Isaiah 9:7).
- ✓ The reign of Christ will be dominated by holiness - Isaiah 1:26-27; 35:8-9; Ezekiel 43:7-12.
- ✓ It will be a reign filled with divine glory - Isaiah 24:23; 4:2; 35:2; 40:5; 60:1-9.
- ✓ Comfort will be beyond description - Isaiah 12:1-2; Jeremiah 31:23-25; Zephaniah 3:18-20.
- ✓ The millennial kingdom will be a time of justice - Isaiah 9:7; 11:5; 42:1-4; Jeremiah 23:5; 31:23, 29-30.
- ✓ The period will be filled with knowledge - Isaiah 11:1-2, 9; 41:19-20; 54:13; Hebrews 2:14.
- ✓ Freedom from oppression - Isaiah 14:3-6; 42:6-7; 49:8-9; Zechariah 9:11-12.
- ✓ Every curse will be removed - Isaiah 11:6-9; 35:9; 65:25.

- ✓ Every deformity will be removed - Isaiah 29:17-19; 35:3-6; 61:1-2; Jeremiah 31:8.
- ✓ The conditions that will exist in millennium will be free from social, political, or religious oppression.
- ✓ All curses will be removed to give way to abundant life, and the venom and ferocity on animals will be removed.
- ✓ Witches, wizards, and evil will be banned, and Christ will minister to every need to give comfort.
- ✓ The kingdom on earth will be united; peace will reign and there will be economic prosperity.

ARREST AND CONFINEMENT OF SATAN

(REVELATION 20:1-3; 9:1-3; 2 PETER 2:4; JUDE 6; LUKE 8:28-31; REVELATION 12:9; ISAIAH 24:21-23)

Before the start of the millennial kingdom, at the end of great tribulation, an angel will come down from heaven with great chain to bind, imprison, and completely detain the devil in abyss, the bottomless pit.

He will be imprisoned for 1000 years so that he will not be able to deceive the nations till the end of 1000 years (Revelation 20:3).

CHRISTS REIGN WITH THE SAINTS ON EARTH

(Revelation 20:4-6; Daniel 7:18, 27; Isaiah 32:1-4; Matthew 19:28; 1 Corinthians 6:2; 2 Timothy 2:12; 1 Peter 2:9; Revelation 3:12, 21)

The saints will sit on the throne with Christ to reign, having the positions and privileges to enjoy.

DELIVERANCE WITHOUT SALVATION

(Revelation 20:7-10)

God is a just God and nobody can find fault in Him.

The reason why He does good to all, delivers the oppressed, and helps the helpless is to prove to the world that He is not partial.

You may be delivered from poverty, suffering, and all physical problems, but if you are not delivered from sin, your deliverance is worse than Ebola and as good as nothing.

Punishment, poverty, or prosperity cannot change the devil or the wicked.

After enjoying from the direct leadership of Christ, full of prosperity, long life, good living, with no disease and war, and abundant provision, people still followed the devil when it was time for decision.

Without deliverance from sin, every other deliverance leads to destruction.

If you are not born again, prosperity alone cannot help you or keep you out of eternal destruction.

If you are not truly converted, you may pretend to be good when there is no suffering and temptation, but at the moment of decision, you will follow the devil whose nature is in you.

No matter how much Satan tries, Christ's kingdom is forever and ever.

THE GREAT WHITE THRONE JUDGMENT

THE FINAL JUDGMENT OF THE WICKED

(REVELATION 20:11-15; ACTS 17:31; ROMANS 2:12-16)

This part of judgment is only for the wicked, the unsaved dead, and all sinners who ever lived and died in ungodliness.

They will be resurrected at the second resurrection after the battle of Gog and Magog at the close of the millennium.

God Almighty, with great authority and infinite majesty will at this time judge unrepentant sinners.

This throne, white, symbolizing the absolute spotless holiness of God who judges righteously according to their works.

THE FAITHFUL JUDGE

(Revelation 20:11-12; Deuteronomy 32:4; Psalms 19:9; 33:4; Romans 2:5-16)

Jesus Christ, the holy, faithful, and all knowing Omniscient God who is no respecter of persons will be the judge that day.

His judgment will be final without an appeal (Psalms 9:7; Ecclesiastes 12:14; Daniel 7:9-10; Matthew 7:21-23; 11:20-24; Hebrews 10:28-31; 2 Peter 3:7, 10-14).

At the judgment day, even the atmospheric heaven will depart, the earth scene of sin will be consumed by fire - 2 Peter 3:10.

THE BOOKS OF RECORD

(Revelation 20:12; Hebrews 4:13; Matthew 12:36; 2 Chronicles 16:9)

These books contain every evil work everyone has done, every evil deed done, every evil word spoken, every evil intent, or purpose entertained.

All the unsaved who depend on their works must appear before this judgment seat to be judged according to their works (Luke 10:20; John 5:24; 1 Thessalonians 5:9-11; Romans 8:1, 33-34; Philippians 3:3).

Those who are saved and their names written in the Book of Life are not going to be involved in this judgment.

THE BOOK OF LIFE

(Revelation 20:12; Exodus 32:33; Revelation 3:5; Malachi 3:16-18)

No sinner's name will enter into this book, not even by mistake, including backsliders.

Your name can be in the church committee's book, prayer team, or even among the list of national and international PASTORS, but if it is not in this book, you are finished.

COMPREHENSIVE JUSTICE

(Revelation 20:12-13; Genesis 18:23, 25; Job 4:17; 8:3; 34:10-12; Psalms 44:20-21; 89:14; Jeremiah 17:10; Romans 1:28-32; 2 Timothy 2:19)

It is wrong to depend on your work or any other work for your salvation rather than the blood of Jesus.

All evil deeds, everything done since the world began by men in every generation goes into record and will be judged.

HELL, THE DESTINY OF SINNERS

(Matthew 25:41, 46; Mark 9:43-48; Luke 16:22-28; Revelation 20:13-15; 21:8)

THE REALITY OF HELL

Hell, which is the destination of the souls of people who die in sin of all ages to the time of the White Throne judgment will be emptied and cast into the lake of fire.

Hell itself is a place of detention with an unquenchable fire.

It existed right from the day Satan sinned and got man involved in sin (Jude 6; Deuteronomy 32:22; Psalms 9:17; 86:13; Proverbs 7:24-27; 9:13-18; 15:24; Proverbs 23:14; Isaiah 5:14-16; 14:15; 28:18; 30:33; 33:14).

Hell fire is a place of eternal punishment and a fearful reality; an awful state and a tragic fate.

WHAT JESUS SAID ABOUT HELL

Jesus spoke about the danger of entering into hellfire - Matthew 5:22, 29-30; 10:28; 18:8-9; Mark 9:43-48; Luke 12:5.

He called hellfire a place of everlasting punishment and an abode of sinners who die unsaved - Luke 16:22-28; Revelation 14:10-11; Matthew 7:15-19; 13:40-42, 50; 22:33.

The Apostles of Christ accepted it as a doctrine - Romans 2:5-9; 2 Thessalonians 1:8-9; Hebrews 10:26-27; James 3:5-6; 2 Peter 2:4, 9; 3:7; Jude 7, 23.

At the end of millennium, all those whose names are not written in the Book of Life will be cast spirit, soul, and body into the lake of fire.

WHAT IS THE LAKE OF FIRE?

(Revelation 20:14-15; 20:10; 21:8; Psalms 9:17; Isaiah 66:22-24)

While hell is the abode of dead souls of all dead sinners; an awaiting trial place of torment; lake of fire is the final eternal home of the devil, his angels, the beast, the false prophets, and all who die without accepting Jesus Christ.

Second death as we see here is the final, permanent, and eternal separation from God, which is also called spiritual death - Ephesians 2:1, 12.

Physical death is just the separation of the soul and spirit from the body - James 2:26.

THE NEW HEAVEN AND NEW EARTH

(REVELATION 22:1-8)

Before we talk about the new heaven and the new earth, let us see divine outline for the last days. Days characterized by a denial of God and Christ; denial of true faith, Christian living, sound doctrine, and the imminent sudden return of Christ to rule the world.

DIVINE PROGRAM OUTLINE

- ✓ The Rapture of the saints - 1 Thessalonians 4:13-18.
- ✓ The great Tribulation - Revelation 6:19.
- ✓ The battle of Armageddon - Revelation 19:15-21.
- ✓ Satan's imprisonment - Revelation 20:1-3.
- ✓ The millennium kingdom - Revelation 20:4-7.
- ✓ The great White Throne Judgment - Revelation 20:11-15.
- ✓ The new heaven and the new earth - Revelation 21-22.

God in His word has promised to create the new world where the saints will dwell forever. After the millennium, God promised to create an entirely new world that will be free from any taint of sin and evil acts.

SETTING THE PACE FOR THE NEW WORLD

(Revelation 21:1-2; 2Peter 3:4-7, 10-14; Psalms 102:25-26; Hebrews 1:10-12; Isaiah 65:17; 66:22)

Because the old earth and the atmospheric heaven have being defiled and contaminated by sin, filled with demonic evil deeds, God decided to destroy them and create new ones - Job 1:7; Isaiah 24:5; John 14:30; Ephesians 2:2.

This present earth and heaven will be rolled away and burnt up with fire and new ones created - 2 Peter 3:5-7, 10-11.

OPPORTUNITY FOR NEW RELATIONSHIP

(REVELATION 21:3-4; 3:12; 2 CORINTHIANS 6:16-18; ISAIAH 65:19)

At that time of this creation, believers will be privileged to enter into permanent relationship with God as sons.

In the new creation, Christ will comfort, care, and relate with every believer closely.

REWARDS FOR BELIEVERS AND PUNISHMENT TO THE REBELS

(REVELATION 21:5-8; 2:7, 11, 17, 26-28; 3:5, 12-13, 21; GALATIANS 5:19-21)

God is determined to make everything new, for the new creations - new heaven, new earth, New Jerusalem, new relationship, new inheritance, and new body.

All things in the new world will be new for new creatures.

THINGS TRUE OVER COMERS MUST OVERCOME

- ✓ The world - 1 John 5:4-5; 2:15-17; John 16:33.
- ✓ Sin - 2 Peter 2:19-22; Romans 6:12-16.
- ✓ Persecution - Revelation 2:10.
- ✓ False prophets - 1 John 4:3-6; Revelation 2:6-7; 15:2.
- ✓ Evil - Romans 12:17-21.
- ✓ Temptation - Revelation 2:26-28; 3:4-5.
- ✓ Satan - 1 John 2:13-14; 5:18; Revelation 12:11.

Deceived people think that to overcome means to succeed at all cost without considering God and His words. To overcome means to prevail, have victory over, and triumph with God on your side - Acts 19:16.

DESCRIPTION AND INHERITANCE IN NEW JERUSALEM

(REVELATION 21:9-27)

THE DISSOLUTION OF THE PRESENT EARTH AND HEAVEN

(PSALMS 102:25-26; ISAIAH 51:6; 65:17; MATTHEW 5:18; 24:35; MARK 13:31; LUKE 21:33; 2 PETER 3:7, 10-14; REVELATION 21:1; ISAIAH 66:22)

God has decided to do away with everything that Satan and his agents have connection with and replace them with new things.

This present heaven and earth haven been polluted, defiled with sin, and infested with demons will be burned with fire.

It is foolishness, ignorance, and myopia to put your trust in the world that is already marked for destruction.

THE GLIMPSE OF THE EVERLASTING CITY

(Revelation 21:9-27)

This is a glimpse of heaven shown to John in his vision as the curtain was drawn and closed.

This is a literal heavenly city; a material one and not mystical as some imagine.

The place is already prepared, waiting for the saints to inhabit as a home - Isaiah 64:4; John 14:1-3; 1 Corinthians 2:9.

All believers who will keep their faith to the end are already citizens of the heavenly country.

We are strangers here on earth and ambassadors of heaven - Philippians 3:20-21; 2 Corinthians 5:20.

Those who refuse to repent and forsake sin will not be allowed to enter the holy new city.

EXCLUSION FROM THE CITY

- ✓ The fearful - Revelation 21:8; John 9:18-22; Matthew 10:33-36.
- ✓ The unbelieving - John 3:18-20, 36.
- ✓ The abominable - Leviticus 18:21-27; Deuteronomy 22:5; Romans 1:18-32; Proverbs 6:16-19.
- ✓ The murderers - 1 John 3:15.
- ✓ The whoremongers, fornicators, and adulterers - Matthew 5:27-30.
- ✓ The sorcerers, witches, and those who use familiar spirits - Deuteronomy 18:9-14; 1 Samuel 28:5-11; 1 Chronicles 10:13-14; Isaiah 8:19.
- ✓ The idolaters - Exodus 20:3-5; 1 John 5:21.
- ✓ The liars - Revelation 21:27; 22:15.

THE INHABITANTS OF THE CITY

(REVELATION 21:2-3, 22-23; 22:3; HEBREWS 11:10, 13-16; 12:22-24; REVELATION 3:12)

This is the city that Christ and the victorious saints will be together in eternally.

It is a literal heavenly city and the capital of the new creation; the dwelling place of the bride, the lamb's wife - Revelation 21:9-10; Hebrews 12:22-23; 11:10.

LIFE IN THE NEW CITY

Believers are strangers here on earth; our home is in heaven where our father is.

Our Savior is in heaven; our home is there; our name is there, written in the Book of Life.

Everything concerning us is there; our treasure, life, inheritance, affections, heart, and citizenship are in heaven, not here on earth.

THE LIFESTYLE IN HEAVEN

- ✓ It is going to be a life of true fellowship - Revelation 5:12; 19:1; 7:9-12.
- ✓ A life of purity - Revelation 21:27.
- ✓ A life of perfect rest - Revelation 14:13.
- ✓ A life of joy - Revelation 21:4.
- ✓ A life of abundance – Revelation 21:6.
- ✓ A life of knowledge - 1 Corinthians 13:12.
- ✓ A life of glory - 2 Corinthians 4:17; Colossians 3:4; John 17:24.
- ✓ A life of service - Revelation 22:3.
- ✓ A life of fellowship with God - 1 Corinthians 13:12; 1 John 3:2; Revelation 22:4.
- ✓ A life of peace - Isaiah 2:4; 9:4-7; Zechariahs 9:10.
- ✓ Specification of the City
- ✓ It will be a disappointment to only hear about this city without entering into it. Hearing about it is not enough; we all need to do everything possible to make it into this glorious new city.

NATURE OF THE CITY

(REVELATION 21:11-14, 18-21, 23; HEBREWS 11:10, 14-16; ISAIAH 64:4; ACTS 7:55-56; 2 CORINTHIANS 12:24)

- ✓ Everything in heaven is transparent; clear as crystal, like unto clear glass, as a transparent glass.
- ✓ One important aspect of the city is that it is full of the blazing, brilliant glory of God.
- ✓ The gates shall not be shut at all; no night there, no obstruction.
- ✓ All the foundation walls of the city are garnished with all manner of precious stones (colored gems).
- ✓ The first foundation was Jasper (clear diamond);
- ✓ The second, Sapphire (blue);
- ✓ The third, Chalcedony (sky-blue agate);
- ✓ The fourth, emerald (green);
- ✓ The fifth, Sardonyx (red and white);
- ✓ The sixth, Sardius (red);
- ✓ The seventh, Chrysolite (gold);
- ✓ The eight, beryl (sea-green);
- ✓ The ninth, topaz (yellow-green);
- ✓ The tenth, Chrysoprasus (green);
- ✓ The eleventh, Jacinth (violet);

- ✓ The twelfth, amethyst (purple).

Because of its transparency, you can see yourself from all points at all times with the fullness of God's glory reflecting from everywhere.

MEASUREMENT AND SIZE OF THE CITY

(REVELATION 21:12-17)

The New Jerusalem is big enough to contain billions of people and as many as will find their way through the narrow gate of salvation - John 14:2; Matthew 7:14.

The symmetry was perfectly designed everywhere in the city.

There are number of 12's noticeable in the city.

- ✓ 12 by 12 gates with 12 angels,
- ✓ 12 tribes,
- ✓ 12 foundations,
- ✓ 12 Apostles,

- ✓ 12 pearls,
- ✓ 12 thousand furlongs and 12 by 12 cubits!

(Revelation 21:12, 14, 16, 17, 21)

The city will be a cube, measuring 12000 furlongs (approximately 1500 miles) in length, breadth and height.

If you take the length and breadth measurements, you will discover that this eternal city will give you 2,250,000 square miles in one layer of mansions!

With millions of intersecting layers of avenues in the city, streets will rise up over streets.

HERITAGE RECEIVED FROM GOD

(Revelation 22:1-5; Psalms 46:4; Genesis 3:22; Revelation 2:7; 1 John 3:1-2; Revelation 21:23, 25; 22:14)

In the city, there is the river of water of life and the tree of life yielding different types of fruits each month.

Is there eating and drinking in that city? - John 21:10-14; Genesis 18:6-8, 16-17; 19:1; Luke 22:15-18, 29-30.

There shall be no more curse, hunger, thirst, sickness, or death.

IT IS IMPOSSIBLE TO PROFANE THE CITY

(REVELATION 21:27; 20:15; 22:15)

Unrepentant sinners will remain forever outside of the city, separated from God and banished forever to avoid desecrating the city.

URGENT NEED FOR REVIVAL

Revival is divine visitation to a people, which brings them from a state of spiritual apathy to a renewed and more active attention to holiness and godliness (Jonah 3:4-10; 1 King 18:31-36).

Revival is a powerful and widespread outpouring of God's Spirit upon people (Joel 2:28).

It is the visitation of God that changes the moral and spiritual climate of a place (2 King 23:4).

When revival comes, weak Christians and dormant churches are revived to be vibrant and militant.

WHY DO WE NEED REVIVAL?

Because many have backslidden and are living a mechanical life without spirituality (Judges 16:20).

Because of God's anger against sin and wickedness God has turned His face away from many (Psalm 74:1-3).

Because of the reign and prosperity of the wicked against the righteous (Psalm 74:4-8).

Because of hindrances and delays in the fulfilment of God's promises and evil changes against the righteous (Psalm 74:9, 4-8).

Because of the increase of many challenges against the righteous (Psalm 74:9, 4; Acts 2:4; 4:13-22).

Lack of brotherly love, increase of hatred, jealousy, division, and prayerlessness in the church (1 Corinthians 3:3-5; Luke 18:11; Samuel 28:6).

Because of the increase of carnality, love of money, lusts, and covetousness (1 Timothy 4:10; Genesis 13:10, 12-13).

Because of the worldly influence in the church, fear of the future, and pride (Hosea 7:8-9; 1 Samuel 8:19-20; 2 King 17:15; Matthew 26:70-74; 10:33; Proverbs 16:18).

Because of the apathy to God's work, God's will, and God's word.

Because many go to church but lack Christian experience and true Christ-like life.

Because many who started in the spirit are walking in the flesh.

We must react urgently by planning for special prayer conferences, sanctifying prayers, and fasting (Nehemiah 1:4; Psalm 126:5-6; Jeremiah 3:7).

Because our strength can no longer carry us through, our efforts and divine investment are under mockery by our enemies.

Many are confused, tired, weak and spiritual dead because of strange delays, lack of God's genuine power and counterfeit in our midst.

Because of promotion of fake, preference of fake, deceits, mediocrity above meritocracy.

Because of the level of hatred, rejections of the righteous above the unrighteous.

Because of the increase of insecurity, violence, evil threats, heartlessness and wickedness.

Because of the increase of refuges, displacements, national crises, wars and mass deaths in our midst.

Because of political crises, backslidings in the church, Luke warmness and lack of Christ like life in the church.

MEANS OF REVIVAL

Waiting upon the Lord - Isaiah 40:29-31.

Diligent study of God's word - Joshua 1:8; Acts 6:4; Deuteronomy 8:3; 2 Timothy 2:15.

Fervent prayers - Acts 13:2-3; Genesis 32:24-26; Romans 15:30-31; 2 Thessalonians 3:1-2; Luke 5:15.

Renewal programs - Proverbs 27:17; Mark 6:30-32; Matthew 17:19.

Desire to know God more - Psalms 42:1-2; Philippians 3:10.

Complete trust in God - Luke 6:45; Psalm 119:60; John 5:30.

Seriousness in ministry - Acts 2:47; 1 Timothy 4:15-16; Colossians 2:6-7; 4:17; Ephesians 4:14; Mark 16:15.

PRICE OF REVIVAL

(Ezekiel 22:29-30)

Denial of self - Matthew 16:24.

Dedication and renewed consecration - Romans 12:1-2.

Continuous prayers, necessary confession and restitutions - Psalm 85:6.

God is searching for people with vision to revive for His work - Habakkuk 1:7.

BENEFITS OF REVIVAL

God's consciousness among the people leading to sinner's convictions, conversions, believers' more thirst for holiness, and fear of God - Jeremiah 9:1.

It brings unity and divine magnetism - Acts 2:1, 6; Psalm 133; Acts 13:44; Ezekiel 37:1-10.

Sinners, backsliders, and weak Christians are drawn back to God and empowered for divine service.

There will be anointed ministrations that will bring mass conversions, deliverances, and healings.

There will be supernatural manifestations, signs, and wonders accompanying the preaching and prayers.

There will be abundant spiritual harvest as sinners of every place, tribe, and religion will be converted - Acts 2:41, 47; 4:5; 6:7.

There will be abiding fruits of the spirit - Acts 2:42-47.

THINGS PRAYER CAN DO

1. Prayers can make nations to start calling upon the name of the Lord (Genesis 4:26).

2. Prayers can make God to accept offerings and remove curses (Genesis 8:20-22, 7:7-13, 16-23).

3. Barrenness can be destroyed through prayers and children can be received through prayers (Genesis 25:21-23).

4. Prayers can save a life, provide water in the wilderness and open spiritually blinded eyes to see and witness blessings (Genesis 21:12-21).

5. Prayers can save you from God's wrath (Genesis 19:1-3).

6. Prayers can bring God's healing upon your life and members of your family (Genesis 7:14-17).

7. Prayers can help you enter into covenant with God (Genesis 26:12-33).

8. Prayers can destroy demonic fears, attract God's favor, defend you from your enemies and draw grace from God (Genesis 32:9-12, 24-30).

9. *Prayers can cause God to manifest in your life, and bring blessings and change of identity to you (Genesis 35:9-15).*

10. *Prayers can cause God to fight for you and break you out of bondage. Then your groaning would stop. Prayers can cause God to remember His covenant with Abraham, Isaac and Jacob, and then deliver you (Exodus 2:23-25).*

11. *Prayers can remove your plagues (Exodus 8:30-31).*

12. *Prayers can cause God to use wind to fight your enemies (Exodus 10:18-19).*

13. *Prayers can divide your Red Sea, cause you to cross without harm and return the same water to destroy your enemies with their chariots, horses, etc (Exodus 14:13-15).*

14. *Prayers can bring provisions for you in times of lack and hunger (Exodus 17:1-7).*

15. *Prayers can cause God to defend the poor (Exodus 22:25-27).*

16. *Prayers can anoint leaders for nation building (Numbers 11:2, 11-30).*

17. Prayers can bring judgment upon all unrepentant leaders and enemies of nation builders (Numbers 16:15, 20-22, 34-35, 44-50).

18. Prayers can cause God to hear your cry and send an angel to deliver you from troubles (Numbers 20:6, 16-17, 21:1-3).

19. Prayers can reverse evil, destroy injustice and secure your inheritance (Number 27:1-11).

20. Prayers can stop oppression and deliver the oppressed (Deuteronomy 24:14-15).

21. Prayers can expose evil, judge the wicked and remove cursed items (Joshua 7:1-26)

22. Prayers can use the moon, sun and other elements to fight your battles (Joshua 10:12-14).

23. Prayers can draw a deliverer to deliver you from troubles (Judges 3:8-9, 15, 2:18, 4:3).

24. Prayers can kill a stubborn unrepentant enemy and save you (Judges 4:18-22, 5:25-31).

25. Prayers can reward your enemies according to their wickedness, evil and avenge you of their evil against you

(Judges 9:1-57).

26. Prayers can give you a resounding victory (Judge 11:32-33).

27. Prayers can revive you from weakness to fight back your enemies (Judge 15:18-19).

28. Prayers can make your life fertile and open your locked womb to bear many children (1 Samuel 1:7-28, 2:18, 20-21).

29. Prayers can defend you before your enemies, if you must fight, and give you victory over your enemies (1 Samuel 7:3-17).

30. Prayers can scatter your enemies in times of war (1 Samuel 11:1-11).

31. Prayers can send thunder and rain to bring fears in the camp of your enemies (1 Samuel 12:16-25).

32. Prayers can save you from evil judgment (1 Samuel 14:38-42).

33. Prayers can make you escape evil plots (1 Samuel 23:1-15).

34. Prayers can cause your enemies to be rejected, killed for

your sake and promote you in their place (1 Samuel 26:1-3, 21-25, 24:16-22, 28:15-24, 31:1-13, 26:25).

35. Prayers can make you recover all your loss (1 Samuel 30:3-21).

36. Prayers can give you direction and promotion (2 Samuel 2:1, 5:1-10).

37. Prayers can cause God to fulfill His promises to you (2 Samuel 7:18-29, 1:17, 1 Kings 5:1-18, 6:11-14, 37-38, 7:1-51).

38. Prayers can convert evil counsel against you to foolishness and kill their counselors (2 Samuel 15:30-31, 16:20-23, 17:23).

39. Prayers can keep you alive to fulfill your destiny; serve your generation according to God's will; deliver you from your enemies; pass over achievements to your children and die in peace (Acts 13:36; 2 Samuel 22:1-51, 1 King 2:1-13).

40. Prayers can cause God to listen to your petitions, answer your prayers and favor you tremendously (1 Kings 3:5-15, Ephesians 3:20).

41. Prayers can humble evil kings, discipline them and

answer the prayers of God's child (1 Kings 13:1-4-6).

42. Prayers can raise the dead to life and destroy unrepentant enemies (1 Kings 17:1-7, 16:29-34, 18:1-46).

43. Prayers can double your blessings and empower you to be great (2 Kings 2:1-15).

44. Prayers can cause God to fight your battles (2 King 3:4-25).

45. Prayers can bring indignation to your enemies to withdraw from the battlefield (2 Kings 3:26-27).

46. Prayers can fulfill God's promise over your life (2 Kings 4:12-17).

47. Prayers can open your spiritual eyes to see hidden things (2 Kings 6:12-17).

48. Prayers can blind your enemies' eyes in the battlefield (2 Kings 6:14-18).

49. Prayers can open blind eyes and discipline your enemies to leave you alone (2 Kings 6:18-23).

50. Prayers can provide a deliverer to deliver you from evil (2 Kings 13:1-5).

51. Prayers can send angels to fight for you, kill your enemies

and save you (2 Kings 18:13-36, 19:1-37).

52. Prayers can cause your enemies to kill themselves in times of battle (2 Kings 19:20-37).

53. Prayers can reverse God's judgment against you; recover you from sickness and prolong your life span on earth (2 Kings 20:1-7).

54. Prayers can cause God to bless you, enlarge your coast and grant you of all your requests (1 Chronicles 4:9-10, 2 Chronicles 1:7-12).

55. Prayers can bring rest and peace in the land (2 chronicles 14:4-8, 15:15-19).

56. Prayers can cause God to fight your battles (2 Chronicles 20:3-13, 20:30).

57. Prayers can cause God to hear a sinner, forgive all his sins and bring him back to his full inheritance (2 Chronicles 33:1-16).

58. Prayers can stop a raging sea (Jonah 1:15-17).

59. Prayers can cause a fish to vomit your destiny (Jonah 2:1-10).

60. Prayers can save you from determined enemies and evil

lions (Daniel 6:1-28).

61. *Prayers can reverse evil decrees, curses and demonic judgment against you* (Esther 3:7-15, 4:1-8, 15-17, 5:3-6, 6:1-17, 7:1-10, 8:3-8, 9:12-32).

62. *Prayers can empower you with a letter of authority to rebuild your war-torn nation* (Nehemiah 2:1-8, 1:1-11, 2:4-5).

63. *Prayers can give you power, determination to build your nation in the mist of your enemies* (Nehemiah 4:1-23).

64. *Prayers can stop wars and evil in your days* (1 Kings 21:28-29).

65. *Prayers can single you out for favor* (Daniel 1:17-21).

66. *Prayers can cause angels to visit you* (Daniel 10:1-21).

67. *Prayers can cause your service to be remembered and rewarded* (Esther 4:1-3, 3:8-15, 9:31).

68. *Prayers can help you to receive the gospel the way it is* (Acts 10:30-31, 1:48).

69. *Prayers can bring down God's presence* (Psalms 74:9-23, 1:8).

70. *Prayers can make Jesus to attend to you* (Mark 10:46-

52).

Of a truth, there is nothing that prayers cannot do, even much more than we can think but there is a condition you have to meet. You must be born again. You must repent truly and forsake your sins (1 Samuel 7:3-4. John 3:18). You must not pray without forgiving your offenders, you must not regard iniquity in your heart (Mark 11:25-25; Psalm 66:18-20; Deuteronomy 1:41-45; Proverb 1:28-32; 28:9; 21:13; Isaiah 59:1-2)

WARFARE SECTION

PRAYERS TO OVERCOME SATAN AND WARS

1. Father Lord, thank You for handing the earth over to man after creation, in the name of Jesus.

2. Let satanic influence on earth be frustrated, in the name of Jesus.

3. Let powers in charge of evil on earth be wasted, in the name of Jesus.

4. Let every evil thing hindering nations building be exposed and disgraced, in the name of Jesus.

5. I break the backbone of Abaddon on earth, in the name of Jesus.

6. Every yoke of Appallon contending with men, break to pieces, in the name of Jesus.

7. Every weapon of the Beelzebub on earth confronting men, be roasted by fire, in the name of Jesus.

8. Let evil powers of the dragon on earth be frustrated, in the name of Jesus.

9. Every messenger of evil on earth, be exposed and disgraced, in the name of Jesus.

10. I destroy the strength of the father of lies on earth, in the name of Jesus.

11. I break and loose the earth from Lucifer's captivity, in the name of Jesus.

12. I command powers of the god of this world to be terminated, in the name of Jesus.

13. Every serpent in the garden of this earth, die by fire, in the name of Jesus.

14. Let the prince of this world be dethroned by force, in the name of Jesus.

15. Every messenger of devil on earth, repent or perish, in the name of Jesus.

DEALING WITH MARRIAGE DESTROYERS

1. Every property of the spiritual marriage in my life, catch fire, burn to ashes, in the name of Jesus.

2. Any known and unknown covenant with spirit husband in my life break, in the name of Jesus.

3. Father Lord, by your power, I destroy every curse placed upon me by my spirit husband, in the name of Jesus.

4. I command the yoke of the domineering power of spirit marriage in my life to break, in the name of Jesus.

5. Let all my spiritual children and evil relationship die by fire, in the name of Jesus.

6. Every written and unwritten agreement with my spirit husband, catch fire, in the name of Jesus.

7. Let the brain of my spirit husband catch fire and run mad forever, in the name of Jesus.

8. As from today, my spirit husband can no longer recognize or reach me, in the name of Jesus.

9. Any evil sacrifice promoting evil marital abomination in my life, catch fire, in the name of Jesus.

10. I break and loose my life from the bondage of spirits marriage, in the name of Jesus.

11. I command the authority of the spirit husband over my life to be terminated, in the name of Jesus.

12. Every destructive weapon of my spirit husband, catch fire, in the name of Jesus.

13. Let all my activities with any evil spirit or group be terminated, in the name of Jesus.

14. Any agent of evil operations in my dream life, fall down and die, in the name of Jesus.

15. Any manipulation going on against my life in the dream, die, in the name of Jesus.

16. Anything enticing me into sex in the dream, catch fire, burn to ashes, in the name of Jesus.

17. Any spirit in charge of intensive sexual thought in my life, die, in the name of Jesus.

18. I receive complete and perfect deliverance from spiritual night raiders, in the name of Jesus.

19. Thunder of God, tear apart my relationship with spirit marriage, in the name of Jesus.

20. O earth, heaven, water, all creature, arise and terminate my spirits marriage, in the name of Jesus.

21. You my private parts, reproductive organ, receive deliverance from evil sex, in the name of Jesus.

22. I take back my destiny handed over to evil powers by my ancestors, in the name of Jesus.

23. Every marine spirit enchantment against my physical marriage, die, in the name of Jesus.

24. I break any marriage with snake in my life forever, in the name of Jesus.

25. All serpentine poison in my life, dry up by fire, in the name of Jesus.

26. Every dragon of my spiritual marriage, stretch and die, in the name of Jesus.

27. Let the anointing of the leviathan upon my life break, in the name of Jesus.

28. Every unclean character, promoting spiritual marriage in my life, die, in the name of Jesus.

29. Any satanic crocodile destroying my physical marriage, die, in the name of Jesus.

30. Every strange fire, burning against my marriage, quench, in the name of Jesus.

31. Any marine spirits sexual agents appearing to me with animal's body, be exposed unto death, in the name of Jesus.

32. Host of heaven, fight for me and deliver me from evil marriage, in the name of Jesus.

33. Fir of God, boil my body against sex in the dream, in the name of Jesus.

34. Any evil personality assigned to deceive me in the dream, die, in the name of Jesus.

35. Any evil personality assigned to feed me to weaken me for sex, die, in the name of Jesus.

36. Any spiritual battle going on against me in the spirit, die, in the name of Jesus.

37. I withdraw my marriage from the altars of my father house, in the name of Jesus.

38. Let the strong hold of my spirits husband collapse, in the name of Jesus.

39. Any obstacle on my way to enjoy my marriage, clear away, in the name of Jesus.

40. I command spiritual and physical divorce between me and every evil relationship to take place now, in the name of Jesus.

41. My spirit husband, concubine, relations and children, die, in the name of Jesus.

42. Any marriage certificate linking me to evil marriage, be roasted by fire, in the name of Jesus.

43. Any invisible marine spirit rings, bangles and chains in my life, I destroy you by fire, in the name of Jesus.

44. Every defeat I have suffered in a dream from spiritual armed robbers, be converted to victory, in the name of Jesus.

45. Demonic spiritual rapist, what are you waiting for? Fall down and die, in the name of Jesus.

BREAKING EVIL MARRIAGES

1. Spiritual sexual abomination in my dream, disappear, in the name of Jesus.

2. Every authority of evil marriage in my life, be broken unto death, die, in the name of Jesus.

3. Every authority of satanic union in my dream, be nullified, in the name of Jesus.

4. Father Lord, commission me for marital success, in the name of Jesus.

5. O Lord, commission me for victory over spiritual sex manipulation, in the name of Jesus.

6. Every spiritual armed robber tormenting me in the dream sexually, I command you to die, in the name of Jesus.

7. I rain the fire of God on the spiritual strongman manipulating me in the dream, in the name of Jesus

8. I rain fire of God on spirit husband disturbing my marriage, in the name of Jesus.

9. O Lord, let heavenly destruction come upon the remote control power used against my marriage, in the name of Jesus.

10. You domineering power of the spirit husband in the dream, I dominate you, in the name of Jesus.

11. Evil effects of sexual relations in my dreams, be reversed, in the name of Jesus.

12. Every spiritual child from evil sexual dreams, die, in the name of Jesus.

13. Thou inordinate affections with the spirit husband, be broken by fire, in the name of Jesus.

14. Every written document in support of spiritual marriage, catch fire and burn to ashes, in the name of Jesus.

15. Evil spiritual union with the spirit husband, I renounce you, in the name of Jesus.

TOTAL FREEDOM FROM LEVIATHAN

1. Father Lord, arise and crush every leviathan power targeting against my life, in the name of Jesus.

2. I break and loose myself forever from every serpentine bondage, in the name of Jesus.

3. Every witchcraft and serpent problems in my life, die, in the name of Jesus.

4. Blood of Jesus, fight my battle now and speak me out of every trouble, in the name of Jesus.

5. By the power in the words of God, I break the backbone of marine witchcraft, in the name of Jesus.

6. Every friendly witch or wizards in my life, roast, in the name of Jesus.

7. Every serpentine poison in any area of my life, dry up and die, in the name of Jesus.

8. O Lord, command deliverance upon my foundation, in the name of Jesus.

9. Every serpent of affliction assigned against my household, die, in the mighty name of Jesus.

10. Anointing of leviathan upon my life, vanish, in the name of Jesus.

11. O Lord, with thy sore, great and strong sword, destroy every marine attack upon my life, in the name of Jesus.

12. Every spirit of pride in my life, roast, in the name of Jesus.

13. Every inherited marine bondage, loose your hold, by the blood of Jesus, in the name of Jesus.

14. Let all the curses in the bible pursue my unrepentant stubborn pursuers, in the name of Jesus.

15. I overcome the dragon, by the blood of the lamb and the words of my testimony, in the name of Jesus.

VICTORY OVER MARINE WITCHCRAFT

1. I bind unrepentant witchcraft with fetters of iron and chains, in the name of Jesus.

2. Every witchcraft battle at the edge of my breakthrough, die by fire, in the name of Jesus.

3. Every witchcraft stronghold in my life, collapse by fire, in the name of Jesus.

4. I withdraw my destiny from my witchcraft altar, in the name of Jesus.

5. Any covenant or curse operating in my life from a witchcraft coven, be revoked by fire, in the name of Jesus.

6. Every dark meeting held against me; receive the thunder of God, in the name of Jesus.

7. Every inherited spiritual handicap because of witchcraft transfer, I reject you by fire, in the name of Jesus.

8. Every witchcraft deposit in my life, melt by fire, in the name of Jesus.

9. Every witchcraft resistance to my prayer, be broken, in the name of Jesus.

10. Let every afflicting fire in my life die, in the name of Jesus.

11. I cast out the spirit of evil inheritance in my life, in the name of Jesus.

12. Every obstacle on my way to progress because of evil rearrangement, scatter, in the name of Jesus.

13. I reject the agenda and plan of witchcraft in my life, in the name of Jesus.

14. I reject the assignment and weapons of the wicked against my life, in the name of Jesus.

15. Every witchcraft decision challenging my household, be disgraced by fire, in the name of Jesus.

LEVIATHAN MUST DIE!!!

1. You stronghold of Leviathan in my life, break by fire, in the name of Jesus.

2. Blood of Jesus, enter into my blood and purge out every Leviathan spirit's deposit, in the name of Jesus.

3. I break every evil covenant that is strengthening Leviathan in my life, in the name of Jesus.

4. I break the hold of every curse, strengthening Leviathan in my life, in the name of Jesus.

5. Anything that belongs to the goodness of my life, presently in the hands of the Leviathan, be released, in the name of Jesus.

6. I frustrate the tokens of Leviathan powers in my life, in the name of Jesus.

7. Every co-operation with Leviathan, I command you to be withdrawn forever, in the name of Jesus.

8. You my ancestral covenant with Leviathan, break, in the name of Jesus.

9. You Leviathan spirit, hear the word of the Lord, die, in the name of Jesus.

10. Every trademark of Leviathan, I shake you out of my life, in the name of Jesus.

11. Every Leviathan spirit competing with my breakthroughs, be chained, in the name of Jesus.

12. Every Leviathan in the river of my life, die, in the name of Jesus.

13. Anything programmed into the heavenlies against me by Leviathan, be pull down by thunder, in the name of Jesus.

14. Every hold of Leviathan in my life, scatter, in the name of Jesus.

15. Any evil mark, that identifies me with Leviathan, be wiped off by the blood of Jesus, in the name of Jesus.

WAR AGAINST DREAM CRIMINALS

1. O Lord, let my due blessings locate me, in the name of Jesus.

2. Father Lord, connect me to the land of my blessing, in the name of Jesus.

3. Any power of darkness that would want to hinder my blessings not to manifest, die, in the name of Jesus.

4. I remove my name from the list of those seeing good things coming but never enjoy it, in the name of Jesus.

5. Every good thing I have dreamt about; manifest by fire, in the name of Jesus.

6. On the mountain of victory and blessings that I am now, I come down no more, in the name of Jesus.

7. The position of greatness that no member of my family has ever reached, O Lord, take me there, in the name of Jesus.

8. Any evil personality that is wishing me to fall; be disappointed, in the name of Jesus.

9. Any witchcraft power that wants me to drift aimless in this world through dreams, die, in the name of Jesus.

10. Every arrow of insanity fired against me in the dream; jump out of me and go back to your sender, in the name of Jesus.

11. I reject every disappointment in my life, in the name of Jesus.

12. Any witchcraft hand feeding me in the dream; be paralysed, in the name of Jesus.

13. I vomit by fire, any witchcraft food that I have ever eaten in my dream, in the name of Jesus.

14. The purpose of God for my life shall come to pass, in the name of Jesus.

15. Any unrepentant evil brain, imagining evil against my future; run mad, in the name of Jesus.

OPERATIONS OF THE WOMAN THAT SITS UPON THE WATERS

(REVELATION 17:1, 15)

1. Every past and present operations of the woman on many waters in my life; expire, in the name of Jesus.

2. Every file of mine with the woman sitting on many waters; roast by fire, in the name of Jesus.

3. Every affliction of the woman that sits upon many waters against my life, die, in the name of Jesus.

4. Any power of the woman on many waters against my destiny, die, in the name of Jesus.

5. Any operations of the woman upon the water against my marriage, die, in the name of Jesus.

6. You the woman that sits upon the waters die by fire, in the name of Jesus.

7. My marriage, reject every bewitchment of the woman that sits upon the waters, in the name of Jesus.

8. My career, reject every arrows of the woman that sits upon the waters, in the name of Jesus.

9. Any re-enforcement and re-grouping from the camp of the woman on many waters, scatter, in the name of Jesus.

10. Oh Lord, I thank you for lifting your hands against the woman on the waters in my life, in the name of Jesus.

11. Any satanic woman in charge of problems in my life, die by fire, in the name of Jesus.

12. Every arrow of confusion from any satanic woman fired into my mind; backfire by fire, in the name of Jesus.

13. Any satanic woman doing business with my brain, die, in the name of Jesus.

14. You satanic woman sitting on my health, release my life by fire, in the name of Jesus.

15. You satanic grip from satanic woman upon my life, be loosed by fire, in the name of Jesus.

UNSEATING THE EVIL WOMAN

(ISAIAH 47:1-15)

1. Any power of the evil woman on my destiny, die by fire, in the name of Jesus.

2. Any power of the evil woman saying that I shall die in this situation, die, in the name of Jesus.

3. You evil woman seating on my finances, die, in the name of Jesus.

4. I unseat you evil woman on my finances, in the name of Jesus.

5. I unseat you evil woman on my favour, in the name of Jesus.

6. I vacate and terminate you permanently on my career, in the name of Jesus.

7. You evil woman seating on my joy, die, in the name of Jesus.

8. You evil woman I bury you alive, in the name of Jesus.

9. I recover every blessings and virtues of mine in your camp, in the name of Jesus.

10. I thank you Lord for empowering me to overpower the evil woman, in the name of Jesus.

11. Any position being held by enemies in my life empowered by the evil woman, die, in the name of Jesus.

12. Anything giving the evil woman the right over my life, be disgraced and be destroyed by fire, in the name of Jesus.

13. I command everything that God created to work against you, in the name of Jesus.

14. Fire of God, destroy all the strength that evil woman has over my life, in the name of Jesus.

15. By the power of resurrection of Christ; satanic woman, loose your hold upon my life, in the name of Jesus.

DISGRACING THE GREAT PROSTITUTE

1. Thou power of the great prostitute, expire, in the name of Jesus.

2. You the great prostitute hunting my life, die, in the name of Jesus.

3. I disgrace and render you prostitute to nothingness, in the name of Jesus.

4. Any ambush of the great prostitute against my life, fail woefully, in the name of Jesus.

5. My life, reject every operation of the great prostitute against my life, in the name of Jesus.

6. Any bewitchment of the great prostitute against my marriage, die, in the name of Jesus.

7. Every diversion of the great prostitute against my future, fail, in the name of Jesus.

8. My life, reject every disgrace of the great prostitute, in the name of Jesus.

9. You the great prostitute, receive disgrace in Jesus name.

10. Oh Lord, thank you for deliverance from the great prostitute, in the name of Jesus.

11. Arrow of God, fall upon the great prostitute and destroy her by fire, in the name of Jesus.

12. You that great prostitute, I command worms to eat up your flesh, in the name of Jesus.

13. I command the judgment of God upon you woman, in the name of Jesus.

14. Every creature arising against the great prostitute, multiply by fire, in the name of Jesus.

15. Let your power over the children of men die, in the name of Jesus.

MYSTERY OF THE EVIL WOMAN EXPOSED

1. Any mystery around you evil woman, be exposed; be disgraced and die, in the name of Jesus.

2. By the blood of Jesus, I nullify every mystery of the evil woman against my marriage, in the name of Jesus.

3. Every mystery of the evil woman surrounding my destiny, die, in the name of Jesus.

4. All mystery of the evil woman against my marriage, fail, in the name of Jesus.

5. My life, be withdrawn from every mystery of the evil woman, in the name of Jesus.

6. Every mystery and evil effect of the evil woman against my life, die, in the name of Jesus.

7. Every mystery of the evil woman against any department of my life, backfire, in the name of Jesus.

8. O God, be God in my situation involving the mystery of the evil woman, in the name of Jesus.

9. My life, be exalted above the mystery of the evil woman, in the name of Jesus.

10. Thank you God for making me to overcome the mystery of the evil woman, in the name of Jesus.

11. Every satanic mystery behind satanic dreams from evil woman in my life, die, in the name of Jesus.

12. Satanic mystery behind the cloth of the satanic woman, be exposed and be disgraced, in the name of Jesus.

13. Every mystery behind satanic staff of the satanic woman, die, in the name of Jesus.

14. Any evil practiced by the satanic woman in my life, cease by fire, in the name of Jesus.

15. By the power of the Holy Ghost, I challenge every satanic mystery in my life, in the name of Jesus.

JUDGEMENT AGAINST THE PROSTITUTE

1. You prostitute, receive the judgment of God and die, in the name of Jesus.

2. You prostitute spreading HIV all over the world; die with your HIV, in the name of Jesus.

3. Judgement of God, persecute the prostitute, in the name of Jesus.

4. Judgement throne of God, purge the life of the prostitute, in the name of Jesus.

5. Any arrow from the camp of the prostitute, fail woefully, in the name of Jesus.

6. Any operation of the prostitute against my progress, die, in the name of Jesus.

7. Judgement fire of God, locate and destroy the camp of the prostitute, in the name of Jesus.

8. Any judgement and effect of the prostitute; be taken to hell fire, in the name of Jesus.

9. Judgement of the woman on water, end in hell, in the name of Jesus.

10. Thank you God for total judgement of the prostitute, in the name of Jesus.

11. Every judgement of the evil woman against me, be cancelled by the blood of Jesus, in the name of Jesus.

12. Let the voice of the blood of Jesus cancel all the evil decree in the heavens, in the name of Jesus.

13. Let the rod of the wrath of the Lord come upon the evil woman, in the name of Jesus.

14. Let the hand of the Lord turn against her, in the name of Jesus.

15. O Lord, make the way of the evil woman to be hewed with sharp stones, in the name of Jesus.

BATTLE TECHNIQUES AGAINST THE EVIL WOMAN

1. Every arrow of the woman of prostitution, die, in the name of Jesus.

2. Every manipulation of the evil woman against my life, be dismantled, in the name of Jesus.

3. Every affliction of the evil woman against my progress, die, in the name of Jesus.

4. Every operation of the evil woman to take me to hell fire, backfire, in the name of Jesus.

5. Every techniques to dig my grave, fall into it and die yourself, in the name of Jesus.

6. Every stronghold of war against the evil woman, I pull you down, in the name of Jesus.

7. Every manipulation of the evil woman to kill me before my time, fail, in the name of Jesus.

8. Any re-enforcement and regrouping of the evil woman against my destiny; scatter, in the name of Jesus.

9. O Lord, thank you for failing every agenda of the evil woman against my goodness, in the name of Jesus.

10. Every chain of the evil woman around my waist, break, in the name of Jesus.

11. Let the angels of God take the evil woman back into the darkness where she belongs, in the name of Jesus.

12. Lord, use the whirlwind to scatter every evil gathering of the evil woman against me, in the name of Jesus.

13. Evil woman, be destroyed by thunder and lightning, in the name of Jesus.

14. O Lord, arise in your anger and scatter every gathering of the evil woman against me, in the name of Jesus.

15. Blood of Jesus, flow into the throne of the evil woman, in the name of Jesus.

CARYING THE BLOOD OF JESUS TO THE FOUNDATION

1. You my foundation, open your mouth and drink the blood of Jesus, in Jesus' name.

2. Any power attacking my destiny from my foundation, drink the blood of Jesus and die, in Jesus' name.

3. Any evil voice, crying against me from my foundation, be silenced by the blood of Jesus, in Jesus' name.

4. Let the blood of Jesus confront and conquer every enemy of my destiny, in Jesus' name.

5. Heavenly Father silence every blood sacrifice crying against me by the blood of Jesus, in Jesus' name.

6. Oh Lord, arise and fight for me by the power in the blood of Jesus, in Jesus' name.

7. Any poverty buried in my foundation, I exhume you by the blood of Jesus, in Jesus' name.

8. Oh Lord my God, empower the blood of Jesus to quicken my foundation, in Jesus' name.

9. Let the host of the demon attacking my foundation scatter by the blood of Jesus, in Jesus' name.

10. Every problem in my life, I destroy your power by the blood of Jesus, in Jesus' name.

11. Any evil power, bringing weakness in to my life, die by the blood of Jesus, in Jesus' name.

12. Let the power in the blood of Jesus arrest every evil in my life, in Jesus' name.

13. Blood of Jesus mingled with fire, enter into my foundation, in Jesus' name.

14. Oh Lord, set my destiny free from every captivity by the blood of Jesus, in Jesus' name.

15. Any power that wants to disgrace me, drink the blood of Jesus and die, in Jesus' name.

BOILING THE WATER AGAINST MARINE POWERS

1. Let the waters in my body boil against every marine deposit in my body, in Jesus' name.

2. Any seed of the marine power planted in my life die by the Holy Ghost fire, in Jesus' name.

3. You my life, catch the Holy Ghost fire and burn every evil in you, in Jesus' name.

4. Let the water in my body boil and kill every disease, germ in my destiny, in Jesus' name.

5. Let the waters in place of birth become too hot for water spirit attacks, in Jesus' name.

6. Every sin my life, drink hot fire and die, in Jesus' name.

7. Any curse placed upon my life by the water spirits, catch fire and die, in Jesus' name.

8. Every stream in this environment harboring water spirit, dry up by fire, in Jesus' name.

9. I challenge the problem in my life by the hot water of God, in Jesus' name.

10. Wherever there I water, oh Lord let it boil against water spirit now, in Jesus' name.

11. Let the waters in the heavenlies boil against every marine powers, in Jesus' name.

12. Let the waters on the earth boil against every marine problem, in Jesus' name.

13. The water spirit of my father's house, drink hot waters and die, in Jesus' name.

14. Let the powers from the waters be chained by hot iron rod, in Jesus' name.

15. I bind and render important every spirit attacking me from the waters, in Jesus' name.

SPIRIT OF MY PARENT LIVING INSIDE ME, COME OUT

1. Any property of my ancestors, inside my life come out by fire, in Jesus' name.

2. Every ancestral yoke upon my life, break, in Jesus' name.

3. Father Lord, take me away from where the enemy has kept me, in Jesus' name.

4. That spirit that no one has challenged in my family, I challenge you now, in Jesus' name.

5. Spirit of my ancestors, living inside me I drag you out by fire, in Jesus' name.

6. Heavenly father abort every evil pregnancy conceived against me, in Jesus' name.

7. Blood of Jesus, conduct deliverance in my life, in Jesus' name.

8. Any power assigned to waste my destiny, be wasted, in Jesus' name.

9. Father Lord, chase away every evil planted into my life at birth, in Jesus' name.

10. Any initiation that has taken place against my life, be broken, in Jesus' name.

11. Let the hand of God taken me away from the grave of my ancestors, in Jesus' name.

12. Anointing to live above ancestral limits, fall upon me now, in Jesus' name.

13. Divine promotion above my ancestors fall upon me now, in Jesus' name.

14. Every evil announcement going on against my life, be terminated, in Jesus' name.

15. Any power attacking my root, why? Be attacked unto death, in Jesus' name.

PRAYER TO GET MARRIED HAPPILY

1. Every anti-marital spirit frustrating my marriage, I cast you out, in the name of Jesus.

2. O Lord, arise and command my marriage to appear, in the name of Jesus.

3. Any evil personality standing against my marriage, fail woefully, in the name of Jesus.

4. Blood of Jesus, speak my marriage into existence, in the name of Jesus.

5. You my life partner, wherever you are, appear, in the name of Jesus.

6. Any power against marriage in my family, I bind you and cast you out, in the name of Jesus.

7. Every adversary of my marriage, be exposed and disgraced, in the name of Jesus.

8. Any power that attacked my parent's marriage, and now attacking mine, die, in the name of Jesus.

9. O Lord, arise and give me victory in my marriage, in the name of Jesus.

10. Any evil covenant standing against marriage in my place of birth, break, in the name of Jesus.

11. Any curse placed upon my marriage, expire by force, in the name of Jesus.

12. O Lord, arise and take my marriage away from captivity, in the name of Jesus.

13. Blood of Jesus, flow into my foundation and rescue my marriage from captivity, in the name of Jesus.

14. Any collective chain holding my marriage in bondage, break, in the name of Jesus.

15. You my marriage, arise and walk out from bondage, in the name of Jesus.

PRAYERS TO DESTROY MARITAL DELAY

1. I anoint my marriage with divine unmerited favors, in the name of Jesus.

2. O Lord, restore every good thing stolen from my marriage, in the name of Jesus.

3. I send the deliverance fire of God into the root of my marriage, in the name of Jesus.

4. Any evil deposit anywhere against my marriage, die, in the name of Jesus.

1. Every unprofitable restriction put before my marriage, be removed, in the name of Jesus.

2. Let my marriage become too hot for my enemies to stop, in the name of Jesus.

3. I loose my marriage from dark and wicked spirits, in the name of Jesus.

4. Any evil plan to manipulate God's will for my marriage, be destroyed, in the name of Jesus.

5. Every anti-marital demon sent against my marriage, be wasted, in the name of Jesus.

6. Let my marriage begin to receive every manner of divine support, in the mighty name of Jesus.

7. Let every enemy of my marriage receive open disgrace, in the name of Jesus.

8. Let every trend of evil directing my marriage be reversed, in the name of Jesus.

9. Any evil head raised against my marriage, be reversed, in the name of Jesus.

10. Every serpent of darkness against my marriage, die, in the name of Jesus.

11. Every stronghold built against my marriage, be pulled down, in the name of Jesus.

12. Let every enemy of my marriage receive open disgrace, in the name of Jesus.

13. Any evil rising from the waters against my marriage, die, in the name of Jesus.

14. Any power working hard to stop me from getting married to the right person, die, in the name of Jesus.

15. I command every household enemy against my marriage to be frustrated, in the name of Jesus.

PRAYERS TO MEET AND MARRY MY MAN

1. Any marriage relationship designed to scare away God's people from me, die, in the name of Jesus.

2. O Lord, help me to marry someone who will be used to promote holiness, in the name of Jesus.

3. Any evil relationship designed to rob me of my place in heaven, die, in the name of Jesus.

4. Let the life partner that will stay with me when I am down or up manifest, in the name of Jesus.

5. Let the partner that will not abandon me when I need him appear, in the name of Jesus.

6. Any power keeping my life partner away from me, release him and be disgraced, in the name of Jesus.

7. Father Lord, empower me to pay any price to get married to your best choice, in the name of Jesus.

8. Lord Jesus, empower my life partner to do everything possible to get married to me, in the name of Jesus.

9. Any power distracting me from getting married to my life partner, die, in the name of Jesus.

10. Let the holy spirit and God's word guide me to marry my best partner, in the name of Jesus.

11. O Lord, use your faithful ministers to guide me to your best choice for me, in the name of Jesus.

12. Let the right partner be strongly impressed in my heart forever, in the name of Jesus.

13. Any evil personality born as a human being to marry me, I reject you, in the name of Jesus.

14. Any handsome person who is not the best choice for my life, I reject you, in the name of Jesus.

15. O Lord, deliver me from the yoke of marital bondage of my father's house, in the name of Jesus.

WARS, BATTLES AND TROUBLES IN MY MARRIAGE, END

1. I speak destruction against every evil voice speaking against my marriage, in the name of Jesus.

2. Any evil structure raised against my marriage, collapse, in the name of Jesus.

3. Any unprofitable comment against my marriage, be silenced, in the name of Jesus.

4. Every enemy of my breakthrough for marriage, be destroyed, in the name of Jesus.

5. O Lord, expose all the enemies of my marriage to death, in the name of Jesus.

6. Any evil power pulling my marriage away from me, die, in the name of Jesus.

7. Let the strange love pulling my partner away from me die, in the name of Jesus.

8. I disconnect any evil relationship attacking my marriage, in the name of Jesus.

9. Any evil personality militating against my marriage, die, in the name of Jesus.

10. Any curse placed upon my marriage, expire by force, in the name of Jesus.

11. Any arrow of shame fired against my marriage, back fire, in the name of Jesus.

12. Any evil shadow in my marriage, disappear forever, in the name of Jesus.

13. I command the author of sin in my home to die with his sin, in the name of Jesus.

14. Every agent of wrong choice in my home, die without mercy, in the name of Jesus.

15. Any evil step taken already in my home, be reversed, in the name of Jesus.

POWER TO CONCEIVE AND BEAR CHILDREN

1. Any physical or spiritual food in my life from any satanic kitchen, die, in the name of Jesus.

2. Eating, sexing and all evil activities of my life in the dream, die, in the name of Jesus.

3. Any evil thing that ever took place in my life in the dream, die, in the name of Jesus.

4. Every vicious cycle of problem in my life, expire, in the name of Jesus.

5. Every sin of my ancestors attacking my conception, release me now, in the name of Jesus.

6. I command the consequences of my personal sins to expire forever, in the name of Jesus.

7. Any evil covenant and curse against my conception, break and expire, in the name of Jesus.

8. Father Lord, correct any evil in my ovary, womb and fallopian tube, in the name of Jesus.

9. I vomit every satanic poison blocking my conception, in the name of Jesus.

10. I break and loose myself from consequences of evil food in the dream, in the name of Jesus.

11. Let the works of bareness in my life be terminated, in the name of Jesus.

12. Any witchcraft instrument that has closed my womb, catch fire, in the name of Jesus.

13. I command every witchcraft poison in my life to dry up, in the name of Jesus.

14. Any curse placed upon my marriage, expire, in the name of Jesus.

15. Any covenant with any demonic spirit known and unknown, break, in the name of Jesus.

DELIVERANCE FROM DIVORCE IN MARRIAGE

1. Any war going on against my marriage, end to my favor, in the name of Jesus.

2. Every agent of divorce in my marriage, be disgraced now, in the name of Jesus.

3. O Lord, help me and my partner to leave and cleave to your glory, in the name of Jesus.

4. I withdraw any position given to the devil in my marriage, in the name of Jesus.

5. O Lord, arise and separate my marriage from divorce, in the name of Jesus.

6. Every yoke of worldliness and extravagancy in my marriage, break now, in the name of Jesus.

7. Any maid or unfriendly friend that wants to break my marriage, be disgraced, in the name of Jesus.

8. Let the spirit of gossip and false prophecy against my marriage bow and die, in the name of Jesus.

9. Any problem in my marriage leading to separation and divorce, be resolved, in the name of Jesus.

10. Any power pulling my marriage out of its rightful place, die, in the name of Jesus.

11. Every thought, plan, decision or desire of divorce in my marriage, be destroyed, in the name of Jesus.

12. Any evil counsel leading my marriage to divorce, be rejected, in the name of Jesus.

13. Every divorce demon sitting upon my marriage, be disgraced, in the name of Jesus.

14. Every agenda of divorce spirit in my marriage, be frustrated, in the name of Jesus.

15. Lord Jesus, walk back into my marriage, rule and reign over divorce, in the name of Jesus.

VICTORY OVER THE ENEMIES OF THE YEAR

1. Any agent of destiny killer sent to me, die on your own, in the name of Jesus.

2. Any evil bullet directed towards my destiny, backfire, in the name of Jesus.

3. Every arrow of death and hell fired against me, backfire, in the name of Jesus.

4. O Lord, arise and take me to my place of rest this year, in the name of Jesus.

5. Any power or personality mandated to hurt me this year, die, in the name of Jesus.

6. Wherever any member of my family will be called for evil this year, blood of Jesus answer for us, in the name of Jesus.

7. I command the wind of judgment to visit the camp of my enemies, in the name of Jesus.

8. Thunder of God's judgment, move and locate my enemies wherever they are now, in the name of Jesus.

9. Let Holy Ghost rain of blessings fall upon every member of my family, in the name of Jesus.

10. O Lord, take me away from every evil trap, in the name of Jesus.

11. I mobilized resources of heaven to arise and come to me this year, in the name of Jesus.

12. I command all my money in this year to meet up all my needs, in the name of Jesus.

13. I command all elemental powers to frustrate my problems this year, in the name of Jesus.

14. I raise God's altar everywhere I go from today, in the name of Jesus.

15. I command my environments to give up all my stolen blessings, in the name of Jesus.

Note of Thanks

Beloved, I hope you enjoyed this book as much as I believe God has touched your heart today. I cannot thank you enough for your continued support for this prayer ministry.

I appreciate you so much for your interest and hope for our nations to dwell in peace and love. This is what this wonderful prayer book is all about. I will appreciate any comment or thought that you might have after reading this book.

Please, do share your testimonies as well. You can email me at prayermadu@yahoo.com, and also in Facebook at www.facebook.com/prayermadueke. I want to invite you, personally, to my website at www.prayermadueke.com, to view other books I have written on various issues of life, especially on marriage, family, sexual problems and money.

I will be delighted to partner with you in organized crusades, ceremonies, marriages and marriage seminars, special events, church ministrations and fellowship for the advancement of God's Kingdom here on earth.

Thank you again, and I wish you success in life.

God bless you.

Prayer M. Madueke

BOOKS BY PRAYER M. MADUEKE

- Americans, May I Have Your Attention Please
- Because You Are Living Abroad
- Pray For Your Country
- 21/40 Nights Of Decrees And Your Enemies Will Surrender
- Tears In Prison
- 35 Special Dangerous Decrees
- More Kingdoms To Conquer
- Prayer Riots To Overthrow Divorce
- Prayers To Get Married Happily
- Prayers To Keep Your Marriage Out Of Troubles
- Prayers For Conception And Power To Retain
- Prayer Retreat – Prayers To Possess Your Year
- Prayers For Nation Building
- Organized Student In A Disorganized School
- Welcome To Campus
- Alone With God (10 Series)
- 40 Prayer Giants
- Prayers For Marriage And Family
- Prayers For Academic Success
- Alone With God- Prayers For Finance
- Special Prayers In His Presence
- Prayers For Good Health
- Prayer Retreat
- Prayers For Children And Youths
- Youths, May I Have Your Attention Please?
- Alone With God- Prayers For Successful Career
- General Prayers For Nation Building
- Prayers Against Satanic Oppression
- Prayers For A Successful Career
- Prayers For Deliverance
- Prayers For Financial Breakthrough
- Prayers For Overcoming Attitude Problems

- Contemporary Politician's Prayers For Nation Building4
- Veteran Politician's Prayer For Nation Building
- Prayers To Marry Without Delay
- Prayers For Marriages In Distress
- Prayers To Prevent Separation Of Couples
- Prayers For Restoration Of Peace In Marriage
- Prayers To Triumph Over Divorce
- Prayers To Heal Broken Relationship
- Prayers To Pray During Courtship
- Prayers For Your Wedding
- Prayers To Pray During Honeymoon
- Prayers For Newly Married Couples
- Prayers To Experience Love In Your Marriage
- Prayers For Fertility In Your Marriage
- Prayers To Conceive And Bear Children
- Prayers To Preserve Your Marriage
- Prayers For Pregnant Women
- Prayers To Retain Your Pregnancy
- Prayers To Overcome Miscarriage
- Prayers To End A Prolonged Pregnancy
- Prayers To Deliver Your Child Safely
- Prayers To Raise Godly Children
- Prayers To Overcome An Evil Habit
- Prayers For Your Children's Deliverance
- Prayers To Live An Excellent Life
- Prayers For College And University Students
- Prayers For Success And Examinations
- Prayers For An Excellent Job
- Prayers For A Job Interview
- Prayers To Progress In Your Career
- Prayers For Healthy Living And Long Life
- Prayers To Live And End Your Life Well
- Prayers For Breakthrough In Your Business

- Prayers For All Manner Of Sickness And Disease
- Prayers For A Happy Married Life
- Prayers To Buy A Home And Settle Down
- Prayers To Receive Financial Miracles
- Prayers For Christmas
- Prayers For Widows And Orphans
- Prayers Against Premature Death
- Prayers For Sound Sleep And Rest
- Prayer Campaign For Nigeria
- Fall And Rise Of The Igbo Nation

Made in the USA
Coppell, TX
18 December 2021